I0454966

CHINA'S EVOLVING SPACE CAPABILITIES:
IMPLICATIONS FOR U.S. INTERESTS

Prepared for:

The U.S.-China Economic and Security Review Commission

Prepared By:

Mark A. Stokes with Dean Cheng

PROJECT 2049 INSTITUTE

April 26, 2012

TABLE OF CONTENTS

Disclaimer and Credits

The authors thank Jenny Lin, Russell Hsiao, and Maggie Rank for research and other support.

About the Project 2049 Institute

http://project2049.net/

The Project 2049 Institute, established in January 2008, seeks to guide decision makers toward a more secure Asia by the century's mid-point. The organization fills a gap in the public policy realm through forward-looking, region-specific research on alternative security and policy solutions. Its interdisciplinary approach draws on rigorous analysis of socioeconomic, governance, military, environmental, technological and political trends, and input from key players in the region, with an eye toward educating the public and informing policy debate. The Project 2049 Institute also provides tailored studies for sponsors with an interest in long-range strategic forecasting. Institute staff are committed to carrying out research activities that meet both U.S. and Asian partner needs for policy change, and public and media engagement.

Selected Acronyms

CAS: Chinese Academy of Sciences

CASC: China Aerospace Science and Technology Corporation

CASIC: China Aerospace Science and Industry Corporation

CCP: Chinese Communist Party

CLTC: China Launch and Tracking Control

CMC: Central Military Commission

CMI: civil-military integration

CNSA: China National Space Administration

COSTIND: Commission on Science, Technology, and Industry for National Defense

ECCM: electronic counter-countermeasures

ELINT: electronic intelligence

GAD: General Armaments Department

GEO: geosynchronous orbit

GLCM: ground-launched cruise missile

GSD: General Staff Department

ITAR: International Traffic in Arms Regulations

KKV: kinetic kill vehicle

LEO: low earth orbit

MUCD: military unit cover designator

NASA: National Aeronautics and Space Administration

PLA: People's Liberation Army

PLAAF: People's Liberation Army Air Force

PRC: People's Republic of China

R&D: research and development

SAR: synthetic aperture radar

S&T: science and technology

SRBM: short-range ballistic missile

SASTIND: State Administration for Science, Technology, and Industry for National Defense

SUMMARY

The People's Republic of China (PRC) has made significant advances in its space program and is emerging as a space power. Senior leaders have established space as a national priority and are allocating significant resources toward enhancing the PRC's space-related technology base. With preservation of its monopoly on power as an overriding goal, the Chinese Communist Party (CCP) bolsters its legitimacy through achievements in space. Policymakers view space power as one aspect of a broad international competition in comprehensive national strength and science and technology (S&T). Investments in space also serve as a stimulant for economic growth. The manned program in particular enhances CCP prestige and draws international attention to the country's expanding technology base.

Without a clearly defined civilian space program, such as that managed by the U.S. National Aeronautics and Space Administration (NASA), the PRC (hereafter also referred to as "China") integrates civil and military uses of space. China's space ambitions are in part peaceful in nature. Yet technologies can also be used with ill-intent. The PLA is rapidly improving its space and counterspace capabilities in order to advance CCP interests and defend against perceived challenges to sovereignty and territorial integrity. Because Taiwan's democratic system of government – an alternative to mainland China's authoritarian model -- presents an existential challenge to the CCP, the PLA relies on military coercion to compel concessions on sovereignty. Although other interests divert attention and resources, Taiwan remains the principle illustrative scenario guiding the PLA's military ambitions in space. Taiwan is a core interest of the United States. As such, the United States should maintain the capacity to resist any resort to force or other forms of coercion that would jeopardize the security, or the social or economic system, of the people on Taiwan.

Space capabilities enable the PLA to conduct military operations at increasingly greater distances from Chinese shores. Greater Chinese competence in leveraging space technologies for military use may complicate U.S. freedom of action in the Asia-Pacific region. Over the next 10-15 years, more advanced precision strike assets, integrated with persistent space-based surveillance, a single integrated air and space picture, and survivable communications architecture, could enable greater confidence in contesting a broader range of sovereignty and territorial claims around China's periphery. Within an emerging concept of a "national aerospace security system," China's interest in space also is driven by a requirement to field countermeasures against advanced U.S. long-range precision strike capabilities expected to be in place over the next 10-15 years.

China has made considerable progress in advancing its space capabilities. A survivable, growing space-based sensor architecture, able to transmit reconnaissance data to ground sites in China in near real time, could facilitate the PLA's ability to carry out long-range precision strikes with growing lethality and speed. Its space-based sensor development is focused on increasingly high resolution, dual-use space-based electro-optical, synthetic aperture radar, and electronic intelligence satellites for surveillance and targeting. The PLA may augment existing space-based assets with microsatellites launched on solid-fueled launch vehicles. The PLA is advancing its development and production of dedicated military communications satellites able to transmit high volumes of data from sensors to a wide variety of users and support operations at increasingly extended ranges from China's periphery. An expanding constellation of navigation satellites further enhances China's operational scope. Beyond traditional space-based platforms, development of "near space" flight vehicles, operating at altitudes between 20-100 kilometers (km), appears to have a relatively high priority.

The PLA oversees a broad and diffuse organizational infrastructure for developing requirements and overseeing research and development (R&D), manufacturing, and operation of space systems. The PLA General Staff Department (GSD) most likely develops joint operational requirements for space-based and counterspace systems. The Air Force, Navy, and Second Artillery Force also contribute toward the development of operational requirements.

The PLA General Armaments Department (GAD) appears to oversee space systems acquisition, including technical design, research and development (R&D), manufacturing, and space launch services. GAD is improving its ability to leverage technical expertise that resides throughout China's defense industrial infrastructure and academic community. The State Council's 863 Program offers an institutionalized extra-budgetary source of funding for PLA strategic technology development. An increasingly sophisticated R&D and industrial establishment supplies the PLA with military space systems. The most important organizations in the space program include the China Aerospace Science and Technology Corporation (CASC) and China Aerospace Science and Industry Corporation (CASIC). As a rough NASA counterpart, the China National Space Administration (CNSA) facilitates international exchanges and cooperative programs with other space-faring nations.

The PRC has prioritized international space-related interactions in order to further political, scientific, technological, and economic goals. China enjoys a broad and close cooperative relationship with space authorities and engineers from Russia, other members of the former Soviet Union, and European countries. China also has expanded its satellite sales and launch services to foreign customers. China and the United States have engaged in limited collaboration in space. Authorities in Beijing have advocated expanding exchanges, despite the mistrust that has characterized the relationship over the last 15-20 years.

The PLA has been investing in a wide range of passive and active means to deny a potential adversary's ability to leverage space-based assets. R&D investments include foreign satellite communications monitoring systems, electronic countermeasure systems to disrupt an opponent's use of space-based systems, and developing the capability for physical destruction of satellites in orbit. Chinese space system development is intimately connected with R&D investment into next generation extended range precision strike systems.

INTRODUCTION

The PRC is emerging as a world leader in space. Managed by a diverse set of military and civilian organizations, Chinese political authorities view space power as one element of a broader international competition in comprehensive strength and science and technology (S&T). With preservation of its monopoly on power as an overriding goal, the CCP consolidates its legitimacy through achievements in space. Adopting an integrated civilian and military perspective in its plans and programs, PRC investment into space technology supports economic development and advances national defense modernization. Successes in space symbolize the emergence of the PRC as a world power. How China intends to leverage its newfound power remains uncertain.

The PRC's programmatic successes in space are significant. Notable achievements include manned space platforms, reliable space launch vehicles, and satellites. China has made substantial progress in developing peaceful and practical uses of space technology. In addition to supplying cost effective international commercial launch services, the PRC's space program supports economic development through subsidized modernization of China's high technology industries, contributing to natural disaster warning and response, and developing commercial applications of space technology.

While the State Council produced space policy white papers in 2000, 2006, and 2011, the CCP's vision for future uses of space remains unclear. China's space ambitions are in part peaceful in nature. Yet technologies can also be used with ill-intent, and military applications of dual-use space technology are a principle concern: space technology increases the capacity of the PLA to project military power vertically into space and horizontally beyond its immediate periphery. Freedom of action in space offers the PLA potential military advantages on land, at sea, and in the air.[1] At present, PLA space and counterspace programs do not appear integrated from an organizational, operational planning, or acquisition perspective. Yet the PLA is rapidly improving its space and counterspace capabilities in order to support CCP interests and defend against perceived challenges to sovereignty and territorial integrity.

Taiwan remains the principle illustrative scenario guiding the PLA's military ambitions in space. Beijing seeks the military capacity to coerce Taiwan's democratically-elected government into a political settlement on PRC terms. Success may require a credible ability to deter, delay, or deny possible intervention of U.S. forces in a cross-Strait conflict. Space assets enable extended range precision strike operations intended to deny U.S. access to or an ability to operate within a contentious area in the Asia-Pacific region.[2] Sophisticated conventional ballistic and ground launched cruise missiles may be an effective means of suppressing regional air defenses and military operations from airbases and carriers at sea. Barring effective countermeasures, the PLA's ability to complicate U.S. access to space assets is likely to grow over the next 10-15 years.

This report examines China's national and military space program. The report first addresses civilian oversight and support of China's space program, including political drivers and budgetary support under national-level science and technology programs. The report then details how GAD is organized to manage space systems acquisition, transport payloads, and maintain space systems in orbit. Discussion then turns to China's space R&D and industrial base, and an overview of selected national and military programs. The report next outlines the role of GSD in developing space requirements and leveraging space assets for integrated joint operations. A summary of China's international space launch services is offered as an appendix.

SECTION 1:

CIVILIAN SUPPORT FOR CHINA'S SPACE PROGRAM

With the preservation of its political system as an overriding goal, the CCP prioritizes investments into space technology for a number of reasons, including the establishment of the PRC as an equal among world powers. Space is an arena for both international competition and cooperation. Successes in manned spaceflight foster national pride and enhance the domestic and international legitimacy of the CCP. Indeed, since the Cold War, space technology has been viewed as a metric of political legitimacy, national power, and status within the international community.

Politburo Standing Committee (2007)
Source: http://english.people.com.cn

Senior civilian leaders within the party and government view space as a national priority and therefore direct significant resources toward the country's space-related technology base. However, space policy, planning, and program management appear fragmented and loosely coordinated among a range of military and civilian players. At an early point in China's space program (August 1989), State Council authorities directed the establishment of a State Space Leading Group to coordinate through the bureaucracy and determine priorities. Its status today is unknown, although a similar leading group exists for China's lunar exploration program. Without an empowered civilian space policy organization such as NASA, executive authority defaults to the PLA GAD for coordinating the R&D and manufacturing of space systems, and commercial and military space launches. As the national executive authority for civil and military space by default, GAD adopts an integrated civil and military approach to managing space programs. In other words, Chinese space systems support both civilian and military users. Development of space technology supports the vision outlined by President Hu Jintao and his predecessor, Jiang Zemin, for the PLA to adopt "new historic missions" to sustain the CCP, safeguard national development, and contribute to global peace and stability.[3]

Beyond supporting political and military purposes, investments into space systems support PRC economic development goals, including transformation of China into an "informatized" society. China's commercial satellite launch business is a source of revenue for the defense industry, and China's remote sensing community may eventually market commercial space imagery to international customers. Remote sensing data can be leveraged for land planning, disaster warning, recovery and response, and weather forecasting.

The State Council establishes general priorities in policy and planning documents, such as the National Long-Term Science and Technology Development Plan for 2006-2020, Five Year Plans, the State High Technology Research and Development Program (e.g., the "863" program), and occasional white papers on space.[4]

The 863 Program is an example of subsidized technology development. China's Ministry of Science and Technology (MOST) has management responsibilities for the 863 Program, with GAD overseeing certain focus areas. Cutting across organizational boundaries, the program creates synergies within China's civilian and defense S&T community. The 863 program has been a funding source for a range of R&D programs, and has served as a mechanism to leverage talent in China's university system.[5] According to one estimate, 70 percent of the members of expert groups that manage individual technology development areas received advanced degrees from American, European, and other foreign universities.[6] Many members of 863 Program expert groups also support working groups managed by the PLA GAD.[7]

Organizations within the space bureaucracy, including the Chinese Academy of Sciences (CAS), the PLA, and defense industry, seek senior party and government support for national-level programs. While a rough counterpart to NASA, the China National Space Administration (CNSA) functions in large part to facilitate international exchanges and cooperative programs with other space-faring nations.[8] Another key civilian entity shaping resource allocation formed in 2002 for space-related remote sensing data is the National Geospatial Information Coordination Committee, which includes PLA representation.[9]

Funded in part by 863 Program grants, China's university system plays a prominent role in space-related R&D. Civilian universities and academic institutions, such as the Beijing University of Aeronautics and Astronautics (NUAA), Northwest Polytechnical University (NPU), and the Harbin Institute of Technology (HIT) have long been engaged in defense R&D. Tsinghua University in Beijing also has been known to be a key player in basic defense R&D. The networks linking China's defense R&D community and traditionally civilian universities appear to be expanding significantly. For examples, Xiamen and Sichuan Universities have been heavily involved in military opto-electronics R&D; and Zhejiang University has been instrumental in developing kinetic kill vehicle (KKV)-related components. Nanjing University has been granted R&D funding for specialized passive stealth coatings for re-entry vehicles.[10]

The PRC government subsidizes technology development, R&D, manufacturing, and launching of satellites and other space systems. Like other countries, the risk and expense associated with the development and manufacturing of space systems require party and government support. China's space and missile industry relies on central government subsidies, although the subsidized proportion of the space industry's budget is unknown.

Since the beginning of its space program in the 1950s, the PRC has prioritized international space-related interactions in order to further national political, scientific, technological, and economic goals. Focusing on space-related S&T, as well as the applications of space systems, CNSA has formed multilateral and bilateral partnerships with a wide range of international partners. Exchanges include cooperative relationships between civilian universities and subordinate research centers with counterparts in the United States, Taiwan, Europe, Russia, and the Ukraine. For instance, a Chinese technical journal credited a major U.S. university with helping the 863-409 working group overcome a specific technical problem related to space interceptor KKV development.[11] Collaboration with Ukraine's Academy of Sciences helped Chinese civilian researchers develop advanced ablative heat resistant materials for maneuvering boost-glide re-entry vehicles.[12]

In short, senior PRC civilian leaders provide policy guidance and authorize resources toward the country's space-related technology base. However, civilian oversight appears to be fragmented, and space programs are loosely coordinated among a range of military and civilian players. National technology plans, such as the 863 Program, are an important subsidy for space technology development. Indeed, China's civilian university system plays a prominent role in space-related R&D, which is funded in part under 863 Program grants. However, in the absence of an empowered civilian space policy organization, GAD integrates civil and military uses of space, and coordinates R&D, manufacturing, and launch of space systems.

SECTION 2:

CHINA'S EXECUTIVE AUTHORITY FOR SPACE: THE PLA GENERAL ARMAMENTS DEPARTMENT

The CCP Central Committee, CMC, and State Council rely upon for the PLA GAD for successful execution of national and military space acquisition policies. The GAD is responsible to the CMC for establishing defense and space acquisition policies, managing China's space program, developing technical solutions to satisfy operational requirements, and overseeing defense industrial research, development, and manufacturing.

Over the past two decades, GAD and China's defense R&D establishment have been breaking down barriers that have hampered the country's ability to field complex space-related system of systems. In order to address shortcomings in defense and space technology development, the CMC directed a reorganization of GAD's predecessor, the Commission of Science, Technology, and Industry for National Defense (COSTIND) in 1998. Part of COSTIND was renamed the State Administration for Science, Technology and Industry for National Defense (SASTIND) and spun off into the civilian Ministry of Industry and Information Technology (MIIT). The remaining elements of COSTIND were merged with GSD Equipment Department to form GAD.[13] Today, the GAD oversees a national-level S&T advisory committee, a number of administrative departments, and operational space units.

GAD S&T Committee

The GAD S&T Committee consists of expert working groups that advise CMC members and civilian authorities on long term technology acquisition planning and space policy and operations. At least 20 national-level technology working groups, supported by defense R&D laboratories around the country, leverage and pool resources to review progress, advise national leaders on resource allocation, and focus resources to overcome technological bottlenecks. Examples of individual GAD-led working groups that touch upon space-related technologies include:

- General Missile Technology[14]
- Precision Guidance Technology[15]
- Computer and Software Technology
- Satellite Technology
- Radar Sensor Technology
- Micro-Electromechanical Systems (MEMS) Technology[16]
- Communications, Navigation, and Tracking Technology[17]
- Integrated Military Electronics and Information Systems Technology[18]
- Simulation Technology
- Stealth Technology[19]

- Opto-Electronics Technology
- Aircraft Technology
- UAV Systems Technology[20]
- Target Characteristics and Signal Control
- Inertial Technology

GAD Administrative Departments

Beyond the S&T Committee, the GAD consists of as many as 10 second level departments responsible for various facets of force modernization, space planning and programming, and space operations. A GAD Space Equipment R&D Center appears to serve as an interface with space system users.[21] The Comprehensive Planning Department appears responsible for overall space-related modernization planning and policy. Space architecture development appears to fall within the purview of the GAD Electronic and Information Infrastructure Department, which is China's leading authority for planning, programming, and budgeting for PLA "informatization" development. It establishes general R&D investment priorities and standards. The GAD Electronic and Information Infrastructure Department consists of at least four bureaus and one program office.[22] The Aerospace Equipment Bureau is responsible for charting the PLA's future space-based communications and surveillance architecture and may manage R&D and manufacturing contracts with the space and missile industry.[23] The Department also has program management functions, such as the Beidou Program Office, also known as the China Satellite Navigation System Management Office.[24]

China's Space Command

The GAD Headquarters Department probably functions as an operational command responsible for space launch, tracking, and control.[25] Managed by the GAD Chief of Staff and operating as the China Satellite Launch and Tracking Systems Department (CLTC), the Headquarters Department oversees China's space launch operations, including Jiuquan, Xichang, and Taiyuan satellite launch centers, and a new space launch center under construction on Hainan Island. Between 1970 and early 2012, CLTC launched 157 satellites for domestic and international customers.[26] The CLTC Director appears to be dual-hatted as GAD's Chief of Staff, who oversees the Headquarters Department.[27]

Jiuquan

Jiuquan Satellite Launch Center, under GAD Base 20 (63600 Unit) supports LM-2C, LM-2D, and LM-4 launch of satellites into low earth orbit, as well as manned space missions on the LM-2F. Base 20 is also a key facility for ballistic

JIUQUAN SATELLITE LAUNCH CENTER
Source: Google Earth

and land attack cruise missile testing.

Taiyuan

Taiyuan Satellite Launch Center, under GAD Base 25 (63710 Unit), functions as China's primary platform for satellite launches into sun synchronous orbit. Situated in Kelan County (Shanxi Province), Base 25 is also a key facility for the testing of medium and intermediate range ballistic missiles.

Xichang

Xichang Satellite Launch Center, under Base 27 (63790 Unit), is China's primary platform for launch of satellites into geosynchronous orbit (GEO). Xichang reportedly the has capacity to launch between eight and 10 satellites a year.[28] Base 27 was the launch point of the PLA's January 2007 test of a kinetic kill vehicle against an aging Chinese weather satellite.[29]

Wenchang

Upon completion, Wenchang Space Launch Center on Hainan Island will serve as a base for launches of heavy payloads associated with the manned space program. The launch vehicle will be transported to Hainan via ship from new manufacturing facilities in Tianjin, rather than rail.[30]

CHINESE SATELLITE LAUNCH BASES

The GAD has a well-established infrastructure for space tracking, control, and surveillance. In order to accommodate its growing space-based infrastructure, China's space surveillance system is gradually expanding in scope and sophistication. Headquartered in Weinan (Shaanxi Province), Base 26 (63750 Unit) likely functions as a space and missile surveillance center, and plays a role in monitoring and identifying debris and other objects in space.[31] GAD's space tracking network consists of a center in Xian, fixed land based sites, at least one mobile system, and four Yuanwang tracking ships capable of operating throughout the Pacific, Atlantic, and Indian Oceans. GAD also operates a number of foreign tracking and control locations.[32]

The Base 26 space surveillance system may fuse data from other sources. One organization possibly supporting the GAD's space tracking network is the China Academy of Science's Space Target and Debris Observation and Research Center, under the purview of the Purple Mountain Observatory in Nanjing.[33] GSD First Department Survey and Mapping

Bureau works in partnership with CAS to operate a very long baseline interferometer (VLBI) network of radio telescopes that support China's space tracking system. Passive satellite surveillance information may be provided by GSD Third and Fourth Departments.[34] China's R&D community also has been exploring options for basing space surveillance platforms in space.[35] During peacetime, GAD Headquarters Department likely directs space operations from the Beijing Space Command and Control Center. Established in 1996, the center appears to be manned 24 hours a day, with a GAD Deputy Chief of Staff serving as watch officer. The facility hosts senior GAD, CMC, and civilian leaders during major events.[36]

Launch Vehicles

The GAD's space transportation infrastructure depends upon a well-established and increasingly reliable family of launch systems to deploy payloads into space for military and civilian users. To date, four basic series of Long March (LM) liquid-fueled launch vehicles deliver payloads to orbits at varying altitudes and inclinations around the earth. The LM launch vehicle family has roots in the country's ballistic missile program, specifically the Dongfeng-4 (DF-4) and Dongfeng-5 (DF-5) intercontinental ballistic missile (ICBM) systems. Based on a March 1965 CMC decision, formal design work on the two missile systems commenced in May 1966. By 1970, initial technical designs were completed. The first DF-5 prototype was assembled in May 1971, and tested from Base 20 on September 10, 1971. Its design was certified in 1973. Both the 211 and 7102 Factory in Sichuan assembled prototypes for testing. The warhead design, however, was not completed until July 1986.[37]

The LM-1, a derivative of the DF-4, successfully sent a satellite into low earth orbit in April 1970, but the program was cancelled the following year. The LM-2 series has been used for delivering both remote sensing and communications satellites from Jiuquan and Xichang Space Launch Centers. The LM-2F is China's most powerful launch vehicle to date, able to boost more than 8,000 kilograms (kg) into low earth orbit. Sharing the same first and second stage as the LM-2C, the LM-3 series integrates a cryogenic third stage that has been used for boosting heavier payloads into space from Xichang Space Launch Center.

Other launch vehicles include the LM-2D and LM-4 series, which have transported remote sensing, weather, and other payloads in sun-synchronous orbit from Taiyuan Space Launch Center. The LM-2D has launched payloads into both low earth orbit and sun synchronous orbit from Jiuquan Space Launch Center.[38] Originally a back up to the LM-3 for launches of communications satellites, preliminary research on the LM-4 series began in 1982, with formal R&D commencing the following year. After the successful launch of China's first Dongfanghong-2 (DFH-2) communications satellites on the LM-3, the main mission of LM-4 shifted to sun synchronous orbit satellite launches.[39]

Since 2008, China has been investing resources into a new generation of launch vehicles, including the LM-5, LM-6, and LM-7. The LM-5 is said to be designed to lift a 25 tons payload to low earth orbit (LEO), or a 14 tons payload into geostationary transfer orbit (GTO).

With R&D beginning in September 2009, SAST's LM-6 is expected to be a smaller launch vehicle capable of boosting 500 kg into orbit. The LM-7 is designed to place a 5.5 ton payload into a sun-synchronous orbit at an altitude of 700 km.

China's space and missile industry also is developing large high thrust solid rocket motors for delivering large payloads. Initial ground tests were conducted in 2009.[40] A two staged solid rocket motor was successfully flight tested on September 25, 2010. While unconfirmed, a large high thrust solid rocket motor with a diameter greater than 2 meters (m) could serve as the basis for a new mobile ICBM.[41]

SECTION 3:

CHINA'S SPACE INDUSTRIAL INFRASTRUCTURE

Senior civilian and military leaders and the GAD rely upon state-owned defense industrial establishments for research, development, and manufacturing of space systems. Administrative oversight of China's defense industry is exercised by the Ministry of Industry and Information Technology (MIIT). Formed in summer 2008, MIIT oversees a restructured and downgraded Commission of Science, Technology and Industry for National Defense (COSTIND), which previously had been a PLA organization that also reports to the State Council.

MIIT's State Administration for Science, Technology and Industry for National Defense (SASTIND) is administratively in charge of defense industrial enterprises that support military-related R&D, manufacturing, and follow-on support. SASTIND seeks to foster greater competition within the defense industry in order to better meet the requirements of the PLA, as well as encourage greater civil-military integration (CMI). SASTIND provides policy guidance to 11 state-owned defense industrial enterprise groups responsible for space and missiles, electronics, aviation, nuclear-related products, shipbuilding, and other sectors.

A key guiding principle is CMI, the process of combining the defense and civilian industrial bases so that common technologies, manufacturing processes and equipment, personnel, and facilities can be used to meet both defense and commercial needs. As a result, spin-on technology is prioritized, as is self-reliance and innovation.[42] In addition, programs that primarily cater to civilian interests, such as China's manned space initiative, may produce militarily useful technologies, such as thermal protection systems and associated materials. Engineers engaged in civilian programs often have more access to foreign expertise, which on occasion can assist in overcoming technical bottlenecks at the component or sub-system level for military programs.[43]

The two industrial groups that make up the space and missile industry include China Aerospace Science and Technology Corporation (CASC) and China Aerospace Science and Industry Corporation (CASIC). As state-owned enterprises, CASC and CASIC receive government subsidies, although efforts have been made to introduce market-based incentives. Led by a group of senior-level executives well under the age of 50, the most extensive shifts in China's research, development, and industrial capacity have taken place within its space and missile (aerospace) industry. The aerospace industry enjoys a historical legacy with a proven record of success, well-established channels and methods for overcoming technological bottlenecks, and prestige needed to recruit some of China's best and brightest. For almost 50 years, China's space and missile industry enjoyed an unrivalled status and priority that has given it an advantage over other industries.

Both CASC and CASIC are organized in a manner similar to U.S. defense corporations, with a corporate-level structure and various business divisions, referred to as academies. Like U.S. defense industrial business divisions, each academy focuses on a core competency, such as medium range ballistic missiles, short range ballistic missiles, ICBMs and satellite launch vehicles, cruise missiles, and satellites. While U.S. defense companies tend to specialize further within a business division, CASC/CASIC academies are organized into R&D and/or design departments, research institutes focusing on specific sub-systems, sub-assemblies, components, or materials; and then testing and manufacturing facilities. Each academy is accountable for profit and loss, and includes an information collection and dissemination institute that diffuses technical information attained from abroad and within China.[44]

China Aerospace Science and Technology Corporation (CASC)

CASC develops and manufactures space launch vehicles, strategic ballistic missiles, satellites, and other space flight vehicles.[45] CASC employs more than 100,000 engineers, technicians, and workers. Its functional business divisions specialize in ballistic missiles and space launch vehicles, large solid rocket motors, liquid fuelled engines, satellites, and related sub-assemblies and components. A new division was established in 2008 that consolidated CASC institutes and factories specializing in inertial measurement units, telemetry, and missile-related microelectronics, such as the high performance digital signal processors and field programmable gate arrays that are needed for long-range precision strike at high speeds and extreme temperature conditions. The CASC S&T Committee advises the State Council, Central Military Commission (CMC), and CASC leadership on space technology issues. CASC's dedicated export management and international contracting entity is the China Great Wall International Corporation (CGWIC).

China Academy of Launch Technology (CASC First Academy)

The CASC First Academy, also known as the China Academy of Launch Technology (CALT), is China's largest entity involved in the development and manufacturing of space launch vehicles and related ballistic missile systems. CASC First Academy is centered in the southern Beijing suburb of Nanyuan. Among its products are China's entire inventory of liquid fuelled ballistic missiles, including the DF-4 and silo-based DF-5 ICBMs, and solid fuelled systems, such as the DF-15 SRBM, and DF-31/DF-31A ICBM. CASC First Academy is also a leading organization in China's manned space program. Subordinate research institutes specialize in guidance,

navigation, and control sub-systems, re-entry vehicles, and launchers. The 211 Factory is the academy's primary launch vehicle assembly plant. CASC First Academy SRBM systems appear to have been made in competition with designs developed by the CASIC 066 Base, and indications exist that it is developing medium range ballistic missile (MRBM) designs to compete with the CASIC Fourth Academy.[46]

Beyond space launch vehicles, the CASC First Academy houses one of the defense technology establishment's most recent organizational innovations – a new design shop focused exclusively on hypersonic cruise vehicles that operate in the realm of near space. The 10th Research Institute, also known as the Near Space Flight Vehicle Research Institute, specializes in the design and development of hypersonic flight vehicles that transit the upper reaches of the atmosphere (between 20 and 100 km) on a sub-orbital trajectory, rather than adopting a traditional ballistic flight path. The establishment of such a separate research institute – one that focuses on a single capability – within China's premier launch vehicle and ballistic missile academy serves as a prominent indicator of the priority that senior civilian and military leaders place on new generation long-range precision strike vehicles.[47]

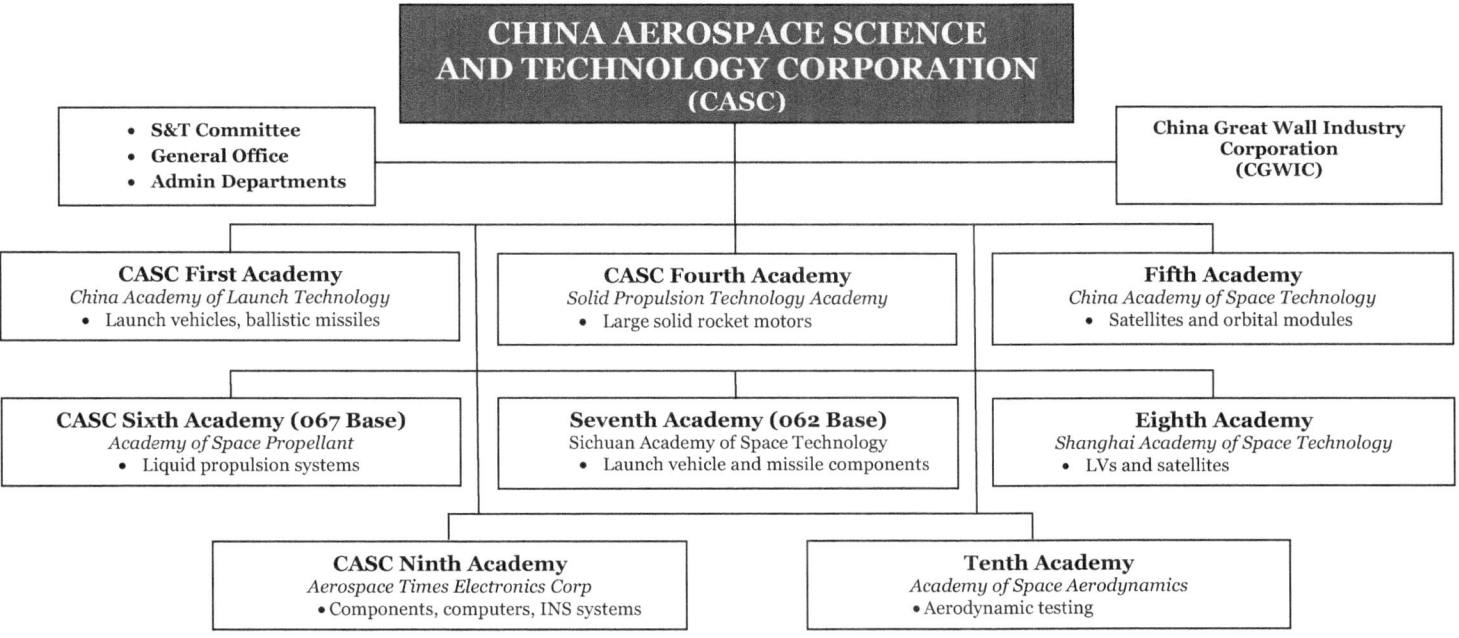

Academy of Aerospace Solid Propulsion Technology (CASC Fourth Academy)

With over 7,000 employees and also known as the Academy of Aerospace Solid Propulsion Technology, CASC Fourth Academy is the key business division responsible for development and manufacturing of solid rocket motors with diameters of 2 m or more. The CASC Fourth Academy is centered upon its design department and has five research institutes and three production facilities involved in all aspects of large, high thrust solid rocket motor development.

Academy of Space Propellant Technology (CASC Sixth Academy)

CASC First and Eighth Academies rely upon a vast supply chain for sub-systems and components. With roots dating back to 1965 and established in its current form on April 26, 2002, the CASC Sixth Academy, also known as the Academy of Space Propellant Technology (or 067 Base), is China's primary organization engaged in research, development, and production of liquid fueled propulsion systems. Originally centered in the Qinling Mountain range west of Xian, the 067 Base employs around 10,000 people in four research institutes and one factory, and is now headquartered in Xian. Among its more recent products include the YF-77 and YF-100, currently China's most powerful liquid oxygen and kerosene rocket engines. It also is a key organization involved in the development of the LM-5 heavy lift launch vehicle, expected to operate from Wenchang Satellite Launch Center on Hainan Island.

Shanghai Academy of Space Technology (CASC Eighth Academy)

The CASC Eighth Academy, also known as the Shanghai Academy of Space Technology (SAST), designs, develops, and manufactures specialized launch vehicles, satellites, and other aerospace systems. Established in August 1961, the CASC Eight Academy is the aerospace industry's largest and most diverse business division. Employing around 16,800 people, the institution was in large part formed through the consolidation of several defense industry research institutes in the mid-1960s. SAST oversees a dedicated design department – the 509th Research Institute – that focuses on weather, synthetic aperture radar, and electronic reconnaissance satellites.

China Academy of Space Technology (Fifth Academy)

Established in February 1968, the CASC Fifth Academy, or China Academy of Space Technology (CAST), is China's primary organization engaged in satellite design, development, and manufacturing. Based in Beijing's northwestern suburbs, CAST institutes, factories, and other enterprises are centered upon the 501st Design Department, which functions as CAST's overall systems engineering organization.[48] Established in 1975, the 502nd Research Institute (also known as Beijing Institute of Control Engineering) designs, researches and develops satellite attitude and orbit control systems, including jet propulsion and various guidance, navigation and control sub-systems. The 508th Research Institute designs and develops electro-optical and other satellite sensors. The principle assembly facility is the 529 Factory. Other institutes specialize in vacuum and cryogenic technologies, antenna systems, and modeling and simulation.[49] A subsidiary in Shenzhen is expected to develop and produce a number of navigation satellites on behalf of the CASC Fifth Academy.[50]

As a final note, CASC's principle marketing arm for space launch services is China Great Wall International Corporation (CGWIC). Established in 1980, CGWIC supplies international customers with satellites, launch services, and other services.[51] CGWIC's stated business goal is to capture 10% of the international commercial satellite market and 15% of the launch market by 2015.[52] CGWIC publications indicate that it is the signature authority for international satellite sales and launch contracts, with CASC Fifth Academy (CAST) and GAD/CLTC as sub-contractors.

China Aerospace Science & Industry Corporation (CASIC)

The second major industrial enterprise engaged in space-related R&D and production is the China Aerospace Science & Industry Corporation (CASIC). CASIC employs more than 100,000 engineers, technicians, and workers within its headquarters, academies or business divisions, subordinate design departments, research institutes, and factories, and commercial enterprises. CASIC specializes in conventional defense and aerospace systems, including tactical ballistic missiles, anti-ship and land attack cruise missiles, air defense missile systems, direct ascent anti-satellite interceptors, operationally responsive tactical microsatellites, and associated tactical satellite launch vehicles. While academies and subordinate institutes appear to conduct independent international business transactions, CASIC's principle export management enterprise is the China Precision Machinery Import-Export Company (CPMIEC).[53]

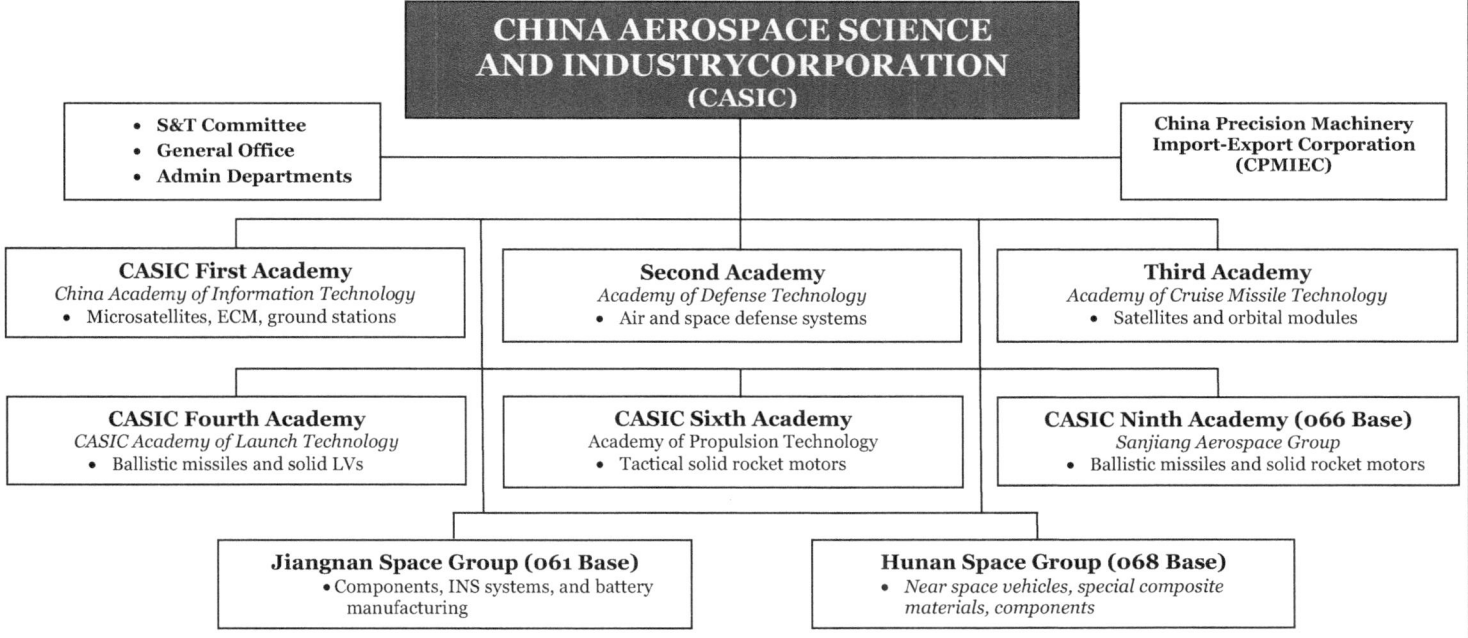

Academy of Information Technology (CASIC First Academy)

CASIC's First Academy, also known as the Academy of Information Technology, has designed and fielded microsatellites. Working with the academic community, CASIC First

Academy is one of a number of entities within China focused on operationally responsive tactical microsatellites that ostensibly could be launched on solid-fueled launch vehicles. It also is engaged in R&D satellite applications and GPS/inertial guidance units. Serving as a test bed for MEMS-based guidance and navigation systems, its most prominent product is the Hangtian-Tsinghua-1 (HT-1) 50 kg microsatellite that operates in a sun synchronous orbit; and the 25kg NS-1 microsatellite. One institute under the Academy of Information Technology specializes in space-based and missile-borne electronic countermeasure (ECM) research and development.[54]

CASIC Second Academy

CASIC's Second Academy is the principal industrial group responsible for kinetic kill counterspace systems, and is China's largest producer of air defense missile systems. Established in 1961, and with a growing emphasis on integrated air and space defense, it consists of a design department, 10 specialized research institutes, a simulation center, three factories, and nine independent commercial enterprises. With the PLA Air Force serving as a core customer, the Second Academy's most prominent defense products include the Hongqi-series of surface to air missile systems, including the missile, radar, and associated ground equipment. The Second Academy also likely designed, developed, and produced the space intercept systems that were tested in January 2007 and January 2010.[55]

CASIC Third Academy

CASIC's Third Academy, established in 1961, is China's premier enterprise engaged in design, development and production of cruise missiles, other aerodynamic vehicles and propulsion systems, and associated launchers. Centered upon the Third Design Department, the Third Academy has 10 research institutes and two factories, with over 13,000 employees. Its traditional core customer has been the PLA Navy. However, its land attack cruise missile program has enabled a closer working relationship with the Second Artillery and Air Force. In the 1970s and 1980s, China's aviation industry made an attempt to enter the cruise missile development and production field. Today, however, it appears that the Third Academy has a near monopoly on the Chinese cruise missile market. The Third Academy is believed to be engaged in R&D on airbreathing supersonic combustion ramjet (scramjet) technology in support of a national hypersonic cruise vehicle program.

CASIC Fourth Academy

CASIC's Fourth Academy was established in 2002 and specializes in design, development, and manufacturing of the DF-21 MRBM and associated variants.[56] Centered upon the Fourth Design Department, the Fourth Academy's business model marks an evolutionary departure from previous aerospace industrial practices.[57] Under its "small core, large collaboration" philosophy, the Fourth Academy specializes in systems integration programs involving a complex supply chain. In the case of the DF-21C, for example, the Fourth Academy oversaw more than 20 sub-contractors, of which less than half were within CASIC.

CASIC Six Academy

In 2002, China's senior leadership directed that the CASC Fourth Academy spin off a major subsidiary located in Inner Mongolia at least in part intended to enhance competition for contracts related to advanced tactical solid fuel propulsion systems, as well as restartable hybrid liquid-solid engines. As a new entrant to the defense market, the CASIC Sixth Academy (formerly a subsidiary of the CASC Fourth Academy) reportedly raised private capital to cover R&D expenses for a new solid motor used for operationally responsive satellite launch vehicles. CASIC Sixth Academy manages smaller diameter motors, including kick motors designed to boost communications satellites to geosynchronous orbit. As a final note, Chinese aerospace engineers have advocated development and fielding of solid-fueled launch vehicles.

CASIC Ninth Academy (066 Base)

The second CASIC producer of ballistic missile systems is the Ninth Academy. Also known as 066 Base, the Ninth Academy was created in August 1969 as a third line industry, specifically supplying cruise missile components to the Third Academy.[58] A key landmark achievement for the Academy was the establishment of a design shop in October 1975.[59] Its most prominent product is the DF-11 short range ballistic missile. Based on a 1993 decision, 066 Base began work on an extended range variant – the DF-11A – with the goal being to double the range but keep the same accuracy. This was successfully flight-tested on August 15, 1998. The 066 Base is believed to have expanded its scope of work, and likely has been developing a follow-on variant to the DF-11A, notionally the DF-11B. Engineers from 066 Base have been cited as conducting R&D into terminal guidance systems.[60]

Jiangnan Aerospace Group (061 Base)

Founded in 1964, Jiangnan Aerospace Group, also known as 061 Base, employs more than 6000 personnel, of which 650 are technicians. Headquartered in Guizhou and with subordinate entities in Suzhou, 061 Base is a primary supplier of specialized missile components and software. Its 20 institutes and factories develop and produce missile-related guidance, navigation, and control software, composite materials, and a range of components, including aerospace-qualified fasteners, gyroscopes, autopilot systems, batteries, micro-motors, and fuel gauges.[61]

Hunan Space Bureau (068 Base)

The 068 Base was established in 1970 in Hunan's Shaoyang area as a third line production complex. Currently centered in Changsha, its core competencies include special materials and components, such as magnets, diamond coatings, and antennas. More recently, the base has become a key center for R&D and production of reconnaissance platforms operating in near space.[62]

In summary, two large state-owned defense industrial establishments are responsible for the research, development, and manufacture of China's space systems. CASC and CASIC are at the forefront of Chinese spacecraft and space transportation development, and play a key role in delivering space systems to civilian and military customers.

SECTION 4:

A REVIEW OF SELECTED SPACE PROGRAMS OF THE PEOPLE'S REPUBLIC OF CHINA

Leveraging the talent that resides with the space and missile industry, the PLA General Armaments Department (GAD) and State Council authorities oversee a range of space programs. Relying on a strategy of incremental modifications to proven designs, China is gradually improving its ability to overcome complex systems engineering challenges and field reliable and cost effective space systems. This section first addresses China's general approach to systems engineering.[63] It then reviews progress being made in China's manned space and other programs, including space-based sensors, communications systems, and launch vehicles.

Overview of Chinese Space Systems Engineering

The GAD and space industry manage research and development (R&D) and production associated with individual programs through a dual chain of command that divides administrative and technical responsibilities. Based on limited available information, contract management and oversight of industrial design, R&D, and production appears to reside within GAD engineering offices.

After authorization to initiate an R&D program, GAD and senior industrial management authorities select a chief designer and up to six deputy chief designers to oversee and coordinate technical aspects of R&D, to include coordinating with a vast supply chain. The chief designer usually is a senior director within an academy's design department. However, a senior engineer from CASC or CASIC headquarters may lead larger, more complex systems engineering projects. Deputy chief designers are generally responsible for major sub-systems R&D and final assembly/manufacturing. Typical sub-systems could include the solid rocket motor sub-system; guidance, navigation, and control sub-system; warhead or post boost vehicle sub-system; and ground equipment sub-system. Deputy chief designers often are selected from research institutes or factories, and not from within the chief designer's departmental chain of command.

The second position within the dual command structure is responsible for administrative program management. The program manager ensures that timeliness and quality control standards are being met; oversees testing schedules; and manages the program budget. Design and program management teams work closely together with GAD and other military and civilian users (CNSA for international programs) to ensure an economy of effort, timely production, and cost effective use of resources.[64]

China's National-Level Space Programs

China's ability to overcome systems engineering challenges is best exemplified by large scale national level manned space and lunar exploration programs. As China aspires to become a leading S&T power, its manned space program has become a vehicle for pushing the limits of human innovation to create new technologies with diverse applications. Manned spaceflights are an internationally recognized symbol of progress and wealth, and China has made considerable efforts over the past two decades to send humans into space as a powerful icon of international prestige

China's first man in space, Yang Liwei, before Shenzhou-5 mission

Source: Chinese internet

and national pride. A number of central figures in national space programs appear poised to assume prominent political positions in the future.[65] No direct link between the manned space program and operational GSD requirements can be discerned. However, national resources dedicated toward manned space programs may be leveraged to enhance militarily-relevant capabilities.[66]

Shenzhou Manned Space Program

Also known as Project 921, Shenzhou is the nation's largest space program in terms of scope and breadth of participation by defense industries. Based on CCP Central Committee guidance, program management of the manned space program was centralized within the GAD's China Manned Space Engineering Office (also known as the 921 Engineering Office). CASC Fifth Academy plays a leading role in design, development, and manufacturing of orbital modules.[67]

However, technological innovation and research have since expanded the scope of its space program beyond military research efforts. These new missions further China's national interests in space, seeking to "explore outer space, and learn more about the cosmos and the Earth; to utilize outer space for peaceful purposes, promote mankind's civilization and social progress, and benefit the whole of mankind; and to meet the growing demands of economic construction, national security, S&T development and social progress, protect China's national interests and build up the comprehensive national strength."[68]

The origins of China's current manned space program can be traced to the late 1980s when Chinese leaders convened a series of conferences to discuss the optimal design for a manned spacecraft. The decision was ultimately made to develop a space capsule, rather than a space plane or space shuttle design, which eventually became the Shenzhou spacecraft. The Politburo, on September 12, 1992, directed investment of resources to support this effort.

The Shenzhou program began with a series of unmanned launches. The Shenzhou-1 launch in 1999 tested the space capsule's control systems and interfaces, while Shenzhou-2 focused on the capsule's environmental systems. Shenzhou-2 also included a sensor package developed by a leading electronic reconnaissance R&D institute.[69] The Shenzhou-3 mission in March 2002 expanded environmental testing, and remained in orbit for six months during which testing of various payloads took place. Shenzhou-4 certified the capsule's emergency rescue systems.

The most momentous event in the history of China's space program took place in October 2003, when China sent then-Lieutenant Colonel Yang Liwei of the PLA Air Force (PLAAF), into space. The Shenzhou-5 flight vehicle orbited the earth 15 times before landing safely in Inner Mongolia. In October 2005, China conducted its second manned spaceflight, Shenzhou-6, to complete the initial phase of Project 921. The program established a foundation for docking a space laboratory, with the ultimate objective of maintaining a larger space station for long-term scientific experiments.[70] The program's second phase, Shenzhou-7, involved space walking as part of the program's mission in 2008.[71] Subsequent unmanned flights included the Shenzhou-8, which was launched on November 1, 2011 and conducted China's initial docking mission with the prototype Tiangong-1 module. The first manned docking mission (Shenzhou-9) is projected for mid-2012.[72]

Lunar Exploration Program

Building upon the successes in its manned space program, China's lunar exploration program represents an empowerment of CNSA as a national space program manager. Based on recommendations from the China Academy of Sciences, and backed by CNSA, China's senior leadership began consideration of a lunar exploration program in 1995 as a focus area under the 863 Program. At least one stated motivation was to explore prospects for mining lunar Helium-3 as a replacement for fossil fuels. GAD's predecessor, the Commission of Science, Technology, and Industry for National Defense (COSTIND), began detailed planning in 1998. In November 2000, the State Council included lunar exploration in its initial white paper on space activities.

Artist concept of Chang'e Lunar Probe
Source: Chinese internet

By 2004, the State Council and CCP Central Committee directed the formation of a Lunar Orbit Exploration Project Leading Small Group to coordinate efforts across the bureaucracy.[73] Along these lines, the lunar exploration program differs from the manned space program. Rather than falling under direct military purview, the lunar exploration program is managed at the national level. Former CNSA Director and current SASTIND Director Chen Qiufa chairs the state leading group. SASTIND's Lunar Exploration Engineering Center exercises day to day program management, along with the China Academy of Sciences' Lunar Exploration Engineering Department.[74]

The program was structured into three phases.[75] Phase I was designed to be a demonstration of its technological prowess, involving the launch of lunar orbiters Chang'e-1 in 2007 and Chang'e-2 in 2010. The mission of Chang'e-1 was the creation of a three-dimensional map of the lunar surface, studying the presence and distribution of useful elements and minerals, and measuring solar winds and their impact on the earth and moon. The 2,350-kg orbiting spacecraft was completed in December 2006 and contained a number of experimental packages. The Chang'e-1 spacecraft orbited the moon for approximately one year.[76]

Launched in October 2010, Chang'e-2 is said to focus on future lunar rover landing zones, surveying of Lagrangian points, and testing of upgrades to the Chinese space tracking and control network.[77] Chang'e-1 and Chang'e-2 were to obtain precise images and maps of the lunar surface and analyze the content and distribution of useful elements and minerals, such as uranium and titanium. Once in orbit about the moon, the spacecraft will take pictures of the lunar surface with a stereo camera/spectrometer imager, including photographs of the northern and southern pole regions; investigate and analyze elements on the lunar surface, to include the locations of large deposits of elements; and take measurements of the lunar subsurface, including measurements of Helium-3 (although rare on the Earth, it is thought to exist in large quantities on the Moon).[78]

Phase II of the lunar exploration program is scheduled to begin in 2013 and is believed to include docking, controlling, and mapping missions. Two remote controlled rovers are to be deployed to conduct surface investigations. Phase III is slated for 2017 with the launch of Chang'e-5 on the LM-5E heavy launch vehicle for collecting samples from the lunar surface.[79] The program has its sights set on a manned lunar landing for sometime after 2025.[80] CNSA has sought private and international sources of funding for lunar missions.[81]

Space Station Program

In March 2011, China published plans for a multiphase construction project to orbit a space station by 2020.[82] Tiangong, or the "heavenly palace," will consist of a main module with two detachable modules on either side. The "Core Cabin Module" module weighs 8.5 tons and is equipped with two docking ports, and will have a two-year lifetime in earth's orbit. This unpiloted spacecraft will be the basis for tests on docking technologies. Tiangong-1 conducted docking missions with the unmanned Shenzhou-8 spacecraft in November 2011.

Two follow-on Tiangong spacecraft are planned.[83] The Tiangong-2 space laboratory, "Laboratory Cabin Module I," is scheduled to be launched by 2013, and designed to test technologies for larger space stations, including long-term living conditions for astronauts. The Tiangong-2 will be able to accommodate three astronauts for about 20 days at a time. In 2015, Tiangong-3 ("Laboratory Cabin Module II") will allow astronauts to remain onboard for

40 days while studying regenerative life-support technology and methods for replenishing fuel and air during missions. The Shenzhou-9 and -10 are scheduled to dock with Tiangong-1 in 2012.[84]

The three Tiangong modules establish a technology base for a fully functioning space station by the end of the decade.[85] At completion, the station will consist of an 18.1-meter-long center module and two 14.4-meter laboratory modules, plus a manned spaceship and a cargo craft. The entire space station will weigh in at 60 tons. Astronauts will eventually take up residence on the station to conduct research in the fields of astronomy, microgravity, and biology.[86]

China's primary motivation for investing in a space station is said by some to support its lunar program.[87] Others suggest that constructing a space station also supports the broader goals of boosting national pride and China's international standing. Chinese officials have stated that the country's space technology will be compatible with that used in the International Space Station, so that modules from other countries will be able to dock with its station.[88]

Space-Based Intelligence, Surveillance, and Reconnaissance

Increasingly greater spatial resolution and an ability to monitor U.S. activity in the Asia-Pacific region (including the locations of US aircraft carrier battle groups) in all weather conditions are likely to enhance China's ability to conduct military operations farther from shore.[89] Space-based sensors also provide images necessary for mission planning functions, such as navigation and terminal guidance for land attack cruise missiles. Over the years, the PLA and Chinese aerospace industry have fielded electro-optical, radar, and other space-based sensor platforms that can transmit images of the earth's surface to ground stations in near-real time. Satellite communications offer a survivable means of communication that will become particularly important as the PLA operates further from China's borders.

A number of authoritative journals have advocated accelerating and expanding China's space-based surveillance system, including the need for a "space-based theater electronic information system" that covers an area of 3,000 square km.[90] Unverified sources indicate that a strategic cueing network for a long-range precision strike capability would rely heavily on a dual-use satellite architecture that is reportedly being put into place ahead of schedule.[91]

A regional strike capability would rely in part on high resolution, dual-use space-based synthetic aperture radar (SAR), electro-optical (EO), and possibly electronic intelligence (ELINT) satellites for surveillance and targeting. China's space industry reportedly is nearing completion of its second generation SAR satellite, and its EO capabilities have been progressing steadily. While information is sparse, indications exist that at least some funding has been dedicated toward developing a space-based ELINT capability. Existing and future data relay satellites and other beyond line of sight communications systems could relay targeting data to and from the theater and/or Second Artillery's operational-level command center.[92] China's aerospace industry has also been investing resources into examining means to reduce the radar cross section of satellites.[93]

Assessing whether or not space systems are under direct PLA or non-military control can be a speculative endeavor. Authorities seldom distinguish between dedicated military and civilian satellites, with systems generally cast as supporting remote sensing, environmental monitoring, or scientific research. Regardless, satellite products controlled by civilian authorities could support military operations. Dedicated military space assets may also support civilian users and natural disaster warning and response operations. Prominent authorities have described dedicated military-use space systems. For example, GAD Aerospace Bureau Director Wu Weiqi has published detailed research on an EO, SAR, and ELINT satellite sensor architecture for targeting of ships at sea. The GSD Second Department appears to operate ground receiving stations for military users throughout the PLA.[94]

The Ministry of Science and Technology (MOST) National Remote Sensing Center oversees China's civilian remote sensing community, coordinates requirements, and manages the procurement of imagery from foreign sources. The Institute of Remote Sensing Application (IRSA) is the primary R&D arm of the National Remote Sensing Center. Even as Beijing fields an expanding array of space systems, it is expected to continue to procure commercial imagery to augment its own sensors.[95]

China has focused its resources on increasingly capable EO satellites employing digital camera technology, as well as space-based radar for all-weather, 24 hour coverage. These capabilities are being augmented with electronic reconnaissance satellites able to monitor radar and radio transmissions. China also is deploying a robust weather satellite capability, oceanography satellites, specialized satellites for survey and mapping, and possibly space-based sensors capable of providing early warning of ballistic missile launches.

Electro-Optical Satellites

The PLA and China's defense R&D community are seeking to field an EO satellite system with increasingly high resolution. China's first experimental imagery system was launched in November 1975, and was followed by two more tests. The system reached IOC in September 1987 when the Fanhuishi Weixing-1 (FSW-1) or recoverable satellite was launched from Jiuquan Space Launch Center, and returned to earth with its film in Sichuan. The FSW-1 provided wide area imaging and orbits for 8 days. Four FSW-1 systems were successfully launched between 1987 and 1992. In 1993, a problem in its attitude control system resulted in a failed FSW-1 mission.

The follow-on FSW-2 satellite carries 2,000 m of film and has a resolution of at least 10 meters. The first FSW-2, also known as the Jianbing-1B, was launched in August 1992, with subsequent launches in 1994 and 1996. One of the more significant aspects of the FSW-2 is its demonstrated maneuvering capability. The FSW-2 orbits for 15 or 16 days before returning to earth with its imagery package. On October 20, 1996, using the LM-2D from Jiuquan, China launched another "scientific survey" satellite that orbited 15 days before returning to earth. The 1996 FSW-2 launch was expected to be the last in this series as China moves to a more advanced imaging system.

In the 1980s, the PRC's space establishment initiated a joint research project with counterparts in Brazil for development of a more capable electro-optical imaging satellite. The result was the China-Brazil Earth Resources Satellite (CBERS) program, which has produced a number of Ziyuan (ZY) earth observation satellites. The ZY series presented China with its first near-real time surveillance capability. In October 1999, China launched ZY-1 (CBERS-1) from Taiyuan Satellite Launch Center. Sensors provided 20 m resolution images that could be transmitted digitally to a ground station over its designed life of approximately two years. Two other ZY-1/CBERS satellites were launched in 2003 and 2007. Second generation ZY-2 satellites were launched in September 2000, October 2002, and November 2004. These were apparently in a lower orbit, offering finer resolution images with the same sensor array. The ZY-2 has been identified in some Western writings as a military reconnaissance system.

With at least 13 launched since April 2006, Yaogan remote sensing satellites appear to be military space platforms designed for EO and SAR imaging missions.[96] The PLA's first EO satellite, developed and manufactured by CASC Fifth Academy, is said to be the Yaogan-2, launched on May 25, 2007.[97] The Yaogan-5, likely carrying another EO payload, was launched from Taiyuan on December 15, 2008 on a LM-4B. As of November 2011, at least four systems demonstrating similar characteristics as the Yaogan-2 and Yaogan-5 satellites have been launched into orbit.[98]

The Shijian-11 series was also developed by CAST's DFH. Specific nature of the vehicle has yet to be determined. The first was launched on November 12, 2009 on an LM-2C from Jiuquan Satellite Launch Center into a roughly 700 km x 98 degree orbit. Among many visions shared by senior engineers within China's space establishment, one is developing an electro-optical camera able to image ground targets with a 0.1 meter spatial resolution. Current state of the art is 0.25 meter.[99]

Synthetic Aperture Radar Satellites

SAR satellites are a core component of militarily-relevant surveillance architecture supporting over-the-horizon (OTH) targeting of surface assets. SAR satellites use a microwave transmission to create an image of maritime and ground based targets. They can operate night or day and in all weather conditions, and are therefore well suited for detection of ships in a wide area. As Chinese engineers have noted, SAR imagery is key for automated target recognition of ships at sea.[100] Processed SAR imagery may depict a ship in various ways, depending on weather conditions, ship orientation and construction, and beam focus. A SAR satellite is also able to image ship wakes from which information on ship speed and heading can be deduced.[101]

China is expected to have multiple types of space-based SAR systems in orbit over the coming years that cater to various users. CAS was active in preliminary research on space-based SAR system in the 1980s, and systems engineering began in 1991.[102] Partially funded by the 863 Program (specifically the 863-308 program), an airborne L-Band SAR capability was viewed as an intermediate step toward a space-based system by the turn of the century. With completion of an on-board SAR image processing sub-system in 1994, China's S&T community and COSTIND approved the final design and associated high speed data transmission system in May 1995. By 1997, the airborne SAR capability was tested and fielded. It was followed by a successful ground simulation system for a SAR satellite program in the late 1990s.[103]

China's initial space-based SAR system was planned as part of a small disaster-monitoring satellite constellation. Under a State Council program formalized in 2003, China has developed a small satellite constellation for disaster warning, recovery, and response. The first phase entailed the deployment of three satellites: Huanjing-1A, 1B and 1C. Huanjing-1A and Huanjing-1B were designed with a three year lifespan. The two EO satellites were launched on September 6, 2008, and the HJ-1C was launched in September 2009 into sun synchronous orbits. The second stage will see the deployment of further eight satellites: four optical satellites and four SAR satellites, which would be expected to increase the revisit rate, thereby expanding surveillance coverage.[104] The SAR satellite antenna was said to be a joint R&D effort with the Russian Moscow Power Engineering Institute's Special Design Bureau (an entity under the Russian Space Agency) and the CAS Institute of Electronics.[105] Like Russian SAR satellites, the HJ-1C is said to operate in the S-Band.[106]

The PLA's first dedicated military SAR satellite likely was deployed in 2006. In development for a decade and launched on April 27, 2006, the Yaogan-1 was launched from Taiyuan Satellite Launch Center. CASC Eighth Academy appeared to have been the satellite's lead systems integrator, and also produced the launch vehicle (LM-4B) on which the satellite was launched.[107] A subsequent system, the Yaogan-6, was launched on April 22, 2009, and at least three follow-on variants have been launched to date.[108] Among these include Yaogan-8, developed over a four year period and, along with the Xiwang-1 microsatellite, launched on an LM-4C from Taiyuan on December 16, 2009.[109] Other possible follow-on variants, designated Yaogan-10 and Yaogan-13, were launched from Taiyuan in August 2010 and November 2011 respectively.[110]

Electronic Reconnaissance Satellites

To augment its SAR and EO systems, the PLA likely has fielded a rudimentary electronic reconnaissance architecture.[111] Chinese military analysts view electronic reconnaissance as necessary to accurately track and target U.S. carrier strike groups in near real time from lower earth orbit as part of China's long-range precision strike capability, including its anti-ship ballistic missile (ASBM) system.[112] Major surface vessels, such as aircraft carriers, have prominent electromagnetic, acoustic, and infrared signatures and large radar cross section. Although controlling emissions from carriers is feasible for limited periods of time, air operations depend on electromagnetic radiation.[113]

The PLA experimented with electronic reconnaissance satellites in the mid-1970s.[114] The satellite was launched from Jiuquan in July 1975 on an FB-1 launch vehicle, which was specifically designed to meet the weight and orbital accuracy requirements of electronic reconnaissance platforms. The FB-1 launched two more experimental satellites in December 1975 and August 1976. For unknown reasons, the program was discontinued. However, technical writings indicate that China's space industry has resurrected the program and intends to field a satellite-borne electronic reconnaissance system. Design studies on an electronic reconnaissance satellite constellation for geolocation of surface targets began in the mid-1990s.[115]

The PLA appears to be investing R&D resources into constellations of two, three, or four satellites using time difference of arrival (TDOA) direction finding or geolocation techniques.[116] Organizations most likely responsible for space-based electronic reconnaissance, such as CASC Eighth Academy 509th Institute and SWIEE, have published detailed assessments of how best to track and target aircraft carriers and other large naval ships.[117] Chinese writings have indicated that while the numbers of electronic reconnaissance satellites are increasing, they have been unable to meet the demands placed on them from different intelligence consumers.[118] Technical studies also have assessed the utility of electronic reconnaissance payloads on satellites in geosynchronous orbit.[119]

Leading candidates for electronic reconnaissance satellites include the Shijian-6 and Yaogan-9 satellites. R&D on the Shijian-6 series of satellites began as early as 2000, with CASC Eighth Academy responsible for R&D and manufacturing of the SJ-6A, while CASC Fifth Academy (CAST) took the lead for the SJ-6B.[120] The Shijian-6A and Shijian-6B satellites were launched in tandem in September 2004.[121] Each satellite pair has a service life of two years.[122] A second pair of Shijian-6 satellites (SJ-6C and SJ-6D) was launched in October 2006. A third pair (SJ-6E and SJ-6F) was launched in October 2008; and a fourth pair (SJ-6G and SJ-6H) was launched in October 2010. Based on this pattern, a fifth pair could be anticipated for launch in October 2012. As a side note, CASC Eighth Academy produced another satellite, the Shijian-12, which was launched on a LM-2D from Jiuquan on June 15, 2010.[123] The satellite was noted maneuvering near the SJ-06F between June 20 and August 16, including a co-orbital rendezvous perhaps for an inspection mission.[124]

Although unclear, the CASC Eighth Academy Shijian-6 satellite series may have served as technology demonstrations. A cluster of three Yaogan-9 satellites, launched from China's Jiuquan Satellite Launch Center on March 5, 2010, appears similar to the U.S. Naval Ocean

Surveillance Satellite (NOSS) system.[125] CASC Fifth Academy's Fifth Design Department had overall responsibility for the Yaogan-9 program.[126]

The GSD Fourth Department may be a leading candidate for managing electronic reconnaissance downlink sites. Space-related units that have been associated with the GSD Fourth Department are located in Beijing, Hainan, and Shandong areas. For example, one source notes that GSD Fourth Department initiated a project in 1999 for the construction of 10 coastal stations in the area of Shidao in Shandong Province.[127]

Oceanographic Satellites

Oceanographic satellites are useful for disaster warning, recovery, and response, support for fishing, exploitation of maritime resources, as well as for military (especially naval) operations. Multispectral sensors may be able to detect ships at sea. The Haiyang-1A and 1B (HY-1A -1B) satellites, both of which were developed and manufactured by the CASC Fifth Academy, were successfully launched in May 2002 and April 2007 respectively. Requirements were developed by the State Oceanic Administration (SOA). The satellites, integrating electro-optical and other sensors, are mainly used for monitoring water color, water environment and temperatures.[128] An initial follow-on variant, the HY-2, was launched in 2009, with subsequent launches expected in 2012, 2015, and 2019. HY-2 integrates microwave technology to detect sea surface wind field, sea surface height and sea surface temperature. Research and development on a more advanced ocean monitoring system incorporating SAR technology, the HY-3, is well underway. HY-3 integrates multiple sensors, such as a multi-spectral imager, synthetic aperture radar, microwave scatterometer, radiometer and radar altimeter. Manufacturing of sensors and satellite frame was slated to begin in 2009, with the first launch scheduled for 2012. Initial requirements call for one HY-3 satellite to be launched every five years (e.g., 2012, 2017, and 2022).[129]

Meteorological Satellites

Since its inception in 1988, China's Fengyun (FY) weather satellite program is another reflection of China's ambitions in space.[130] China's meteorological satellite program began with Chinese Premier Zhou Enlai's 1970 approval of a CMC proposal to initiate R&D on weather satellites.[131] With the launch of the first FY-1A in 1988, China became the third nation to launch its own meteorological satellites. Since then, the PRC has launched four FY-1 weather satellites into polar orbit, five FY-2 geosynchronous weather satellites, and two FY-3 satellites that were boosted into polar orbits on Long March-4 launch vehicles.

The FY series appear to be roughly analogous to those associated with the U.S Defense Meteorological Satellite Program (DMSP). The FY-3, equipped with almost a dozen all weather sensors, is China's most advanced space asset providing meteorological support to PLA and other users. The system also could provide measurement and signature intelligence (MASINT) data to China's emerging ASBM targeting architecture.[132] In addition to five additional FY-3 satellites to be launched between now and 2020, the next generation geosynchronous weather satellite, the FY-4, is expected to enter service in 2014.[133]

As a dual-use asset, FY-3 requirements appear to have been developed by both the PLA General Staff Department (GSD) and China Meteorological Bureau. Specific PLA users with significant interests in the program include the GSD Second Department and GSD Third Department. Presumably, the GSD Operations Department and Service-level weather bureaus are key PLA users.

The R&D and manufacturing supply chain have stretched across a range of bureaucracies. The CASC Eighth Academy is the lead systems integrator for the satellites, launch vehicle, and ground system R&D. Overall system designers were SAST's Sun Jingliang and Meng Zhizhong.[134] Lead satellite sub-system designer was SAST's Dong Yaohai.[135] Shanghai Institute of Technical Physics appears to have been responsible for the hyperspectral infrared sensor.

The GSD Third Department 57 Research Institute, supported by the China Electronics Technology Group Corporation (CETC) 39th Research Institute (Northwest Institute of Electronic Equipment), developed the ground based receiving antenna system for the FY-3.[136] Ground stations responsible for managing FY-3 satellite data reception, transmission and processing are located in Urumqi, Guangzhou, and Jiamusi.[137]

Other sub-contractors include SAST's Shanghai Institute of Electronic and Communications Equipment (804th Research Institute), CASC Fifth Academy's Beijing Institute of Satellite Information Engineering (503rd Research Institute), and the CMA's Network Surveillance Division.[138] The FY-3 satellite carries at least 11 on-board sensors.[139] One study noted that the FY-3 includes a prototype package intended to support other sensors, such as OTH radar systems, to compensate for sea clutter when tracking aircraft carriers and other moving targets at sea. Greater resolution enables more precise targeting.[140]

In short, Fengyun satellites collect and provide strategic weather reconnaissance data for civilian and military purposes. An accurate assessment of current and future weather conditions, such as cloud cover, atmospheric moisture, winds, temperature, and ocean currents, is critical for a range of military operations. Weather satellites can measure electromagnetic conditions in the ionosphere that could affect OTH radar and communication systems. They also can provide militarily useful data associated with complex maritime environments and terrains, including observation of targets under camouflage or perhaps even underground.

Ballistic Missile Warning Infrared Satellites

Space-based assets with infrared sensors are utilized to detect hot plumes from ballistic missiles, and other heat sources. The first U.S. missile early warning system, MIDAS, was launched in the early 1960s and was followed by Defense Support Program (DSP) satellites in the early 1970s. DSP satellites use infrared telescopes, backed by an optical component, in a geosynchronous orbit to maintain constant surveillance. The former Soviet space-based early warning system, completed in 1982, used a constellation of satellites in highly elliptical Molniya orbits to the same effect.

Chinese engineers have indicated interest in ballistic missile early warning satellites, at least in part for purposes of countermeasures against U.S. DSP and space tracking and surveillance system (SBIRS).[141] Detection of ballistic missiles launches while in the boost phase could facilitate cueing of missile defense radar systems. No firm evidence exists that China has deployed a space-based ballistic missile early warning capability. However, a technical foundation exists: for example, with infrared sensors associated with the FY weather satellite program.[142] The SJ-7 satellite, designed and developed by SAST's 509 Research Institute and launched on a SAST-manufactured LM-2D from Jiuquan on July 6, 2005, has been cited as an experimental platform to test pushbroom and mercury-cadmium-telluride (HgCdTe) infrared sensor arrays.[143] Also equipped with a star sensor for precise attitude control, the SJ-7 took only 33 months to design and develop from its initiation in August 2002.[144] The CAS Shanghai Institute of Technical Physics is said to have developed the infrared sensors.[145]

Survey and Mapping Satellites

Military geodesy has long been important for determining precise positions of points on the earth's surface for mapping and to support ballistic missile operations. Scientific applications, such as determining the precise size and shape of the earth have become increasingly important for satellite tracking, global navigation, and missile defense operations. China's first digital imaging system capable of stereo Earth-terrain mapping was the Shiyan-1, also referred to as Tansuo-1, which was launched in 2004 on an LM-2C. The 300kg Shiyan 2 (Tansuo-2) was launched on an LM-2C on November 18, 2004, with a third (Shiyan-3) launched in 2008 on an LM-2D.[146] With R&D beginning in March 2008, a dedicated survey and mapping satellite – the ZY-3 – was launched on an LM-4B from Taiyuan in January 2012. Presumably, the satellite would be capable of three dimensional digital terrain imaging.[147]

Space-Based Communications and Navigation Satellite Systems

Space-based platforms are a critical means of communicating over the horizon. The PLA appears to be applying principles of network centric warfare to communicate and correlate data from increasingly sophisticated sensor architecture. Network-centric warfare equips soldiers, airmen, and soldiers with a common operational picture that significantly increases situational awareness. As a result, individuals and units equipped to participate in the network are able to synchronize action without necessarily having to wait for orders, which in turn reduces their reaction time. In addition, the network allows for dispersed and flexible operations at lower cost. Therefore, the introduction of a networked common tactical picture based on an advanced tactical data link program is a paradigm shift that could gradually break down the PLA's traditionally stovepiped, service-oriented approach to defense.[148]

Communications Satellites

China has long had an interest in communications satellites, with one initial motivation being to raise the level of education for China's masses.[149] Since the launch of its first experimental communications satellite in January 1984 and the first operational system in March 1988, China's communications satellite capacity has grown in sophistication. As many as nine commercial communications satellites are owned or operated by organizations in China.[150] Before the development and launch of dedicated military communications satellites, the PLA most likely leased civilian transponders operating in the C- and Ku-bands, such as SinoSat and ChinaSat.

CASC Fifth Academy (CAST) is the industrial lead systems integrator for major communications satellite programs. CAST's latest generation communications satellite, the DFH-4, is a larger, heavier payload with L- and Ka-band transponders.[151] Leveraging successes with the DFH-4 telecommunications satellite, the PLA appears to have invested in dedicated military communication satellites, including the Fenghuo-1 and Shentong systems. Fenghuo-1, also known as ChinaSat-22, was launched in January 2000 and functioned as the PLA's first dedicated military communications satellite. Weighing 2,300 kg and designed to operate for eight years, Fenghuo-2 (Chinasat-22A) was launched in September 2006. Shentong-1, also known as ChinaSat-20, was launched in November 2003, and is said to incorporate steerable spot beams operating in the Ku Band. Shentong-2 (ChinaSat-20A) was launched on November 25, 2010.[152]

Data Relay Satellites

To expand the scope of its communications satellite architecture, China has been developing a data relay capability. China's first generation data relay satellite, the Tianlian-1, was launched in April 2008 and a second in July 2011. Theoretically, the satellites, using a basic DFH-3 bus, support the manned space program. The satellites also could allow sensors to operate beyond line of sight of ground stations in China.[153] Engineers have developed concepts for an even more sophisticated data relay architecture in the future.[154]

Navigation Satellites

Navigation satellites are another important aspect of China's space development. China's first generation navigation satellite system, the Beidou-1, consisted of two geosynchronous satellites (plus spares) for civil and military purposes and was limited to coverage within the Asia-Pacific region. This was an active location system, with a signal from a handheld unit transmitted to the two geosynchronous satellites, which then transmitted the signal to an earth station. The earth station measured the differential in the two signals (one per satellite), determined the location that fit, and then transmitted that data back to the handheld unit.

Planning for a second generation of navigation satellites, Beidou-2 (Compass), began in April 1999 under sponsorship of GSD First Department and with participation from civilian entities. This system was closer to the GPS and the Russian GLONASS system, with passive receivers receiving signals from an array of medium earth orbit satellites. The eighth Beidou-2 satellite was launched from Xichang Satellite Launch Center in April 2011, with another 24 satellites expected. An emphasis was placed on system survivability, division of military and civilian bandwidth usage, laser ranging, and integration of micro-electro-mechanical system (MEMS) technology.[155] A CASC subsidiary in Shenzhen has also played a role in navigation satellite production.[156]

The Beidou system was initially associated with the European Union (EU) on the Galileo navigation satellite system, an alternative to the GPS. The Chinese, however, were apparently excluded from various aspects of the program, including key software components, and were given only limited workshare. Consequently, the Beidou-2 system may be seen as the Chinese answer to the now delayed European program. The GSD First Department Survey and Mapping Bureau is the primary military organization responsible for the ground segment of China's satellite navigation system.[157]

Microsatellite Programs

In a crisis situation, China may have the option of augmenting existing space-based assets with microsatellites launched on solid-fueled launch vehicles. Weighing between 10 and 100 kg, microsatellite programs to date appear experimental in nature, but competency and experience could translate into a lower cost, operationally responsive space capability.[158] Microsatellites also serve as experimental technology test beds for MEMS, and formational flight as an integrated constellation that could offer greater survivability due to numbers and potentially reduced radar cross section. Microsatellites also have been viewed as technology demonstrations for counterspace operations, including ASAT kinetic kill vehicles. A number of R&D organizations in China have entered the microsatellite field, including CAS, CASIC First, CASC Fifth, and CASC Eighth Academies, Nanjing University of Aeronautics and Astronautics (NUAA), Harbin Institute of Technology (HIT), and Qinghua and Zhejiang Universities.[159]

Initial technology demonstration programs include the Tsinghua-1 satellite, an ostensibly private-funded program carried out in conjunction with the UK's University of Surrey. Launched in June 2000, the Tsinghua-1 weighed 50 kg and conducted experiments on satellite-borne navigation, multispectral remote sensing, and store and dump downlink communications.[160] The program appears to have been jointly managed by Tsinghua University and CASIC First Academy.[161] A subsequent Tsinghua/CASIC microsatellite program was the Naxing-1, launched on April 18, 2004 as a piggyback to the Shiyan-1. Naxing served as a MEMS test bed for an on-board miniature inertial measurement unit (MIMU) and

CMOS digital imagery.[162] Shiyan-1, developed by the Harbin Institute of Technology, was also launched on April 18, 2004 and followed by the Shiyan-3. Other organizations involved include CAST, CAS Changchun Institute of Opto-Electronics, and Xian Institute of Survey and Mapping.[163]

Another is the Pixing-1 microsatellite, a state-funded completed program developed by Zhejiang University, which has been involved in defense-related basic research.[164] The initial Pixing satellite was launched from Jiuquan in conjunction with the Yaogan-2 on May 25, 2007. Two additional Pixing microsatellites were launched as piggyback payloads on the Yaogan-11 in September 22, 2010 from Jiuquan. The satellite was intended to function as a test platform for digital imagery, data storage and management; downlink communications, attitude control; MEMS inertial measurement unit, thermal control, and other missions.[165]

Other programs include Banxing-1 (BX-1), a payload of less than 40 kg that deployed from the Shenzhou-7 orbital module in September 2008 to test data relay and other payloads associated with Shenzhou-8. The BX-1 satellite was designed and manufactured by CAS's Satellite Engineering Center. Another system, the 88 kg Chuangxin-1 (CX-1) satellite, was a prototype low earth orbit telecommunication satellite that was launched in October 2003. A second was launched in November 2008.[166] Yet another program is the Beijing-1, a miniature satellite designed and manufactured by the Surrey Satellite Technology Ltd (SSTL) for the Disaster Monitoring Constellation (DMC) of the International Charter on Space and Major Disasters. Beijing-1 was delivered into polar orbit on a Russian launch vehicle from Plesetsk in October 2005. SSTL concluded an agreement for three additional satellites with one meter resolution to be launched in 2014.[167]

Chinese entities have also been investing resources into placing microsatellites into orbit with operationally responsive solid fuelled systems. Development of an operationally responsive launch vehicle appears to be one of the most ambitious efforts by China's aerospace industry to field a product through privately raised funds, at least in its initial phase.[168] The CASIC Fourth Academy developed the Kaituozhe (KT) small launch vehicle in order to serve the domestic and foreign market for boosting small and microsatellites with weights less that 100 kg into low earth orbit. The developmental program is said to have begun in June 2000, with the third-stage motor successfully tested on February 25, 2001.

The KT-1 was self-financed by CASIC and is said to be capable of delivering a 50 kg payload to a 400 km altitude sun-synchronous orbit.[169] Aerospace industry reporting indicated that an initial test on the 1.4 m diameter first stage motor on September 15, 2002 failed to achieve the anticipated outcome. The test involved the launch of the 35.8 kg KT-1PS microsatellite, manufactured by CASIC First Academy, from Taiyuan Satellite Launch Center into an intended 300 km altitude orbit.[170]

Citing obstacles to continuing the program after the initial failure, there are conflicting reports regarding subsequent tests. *China Space News* reported that a September 16, 2003 test launch of the four-staged KT-1 launch vehicle was successful. Launching a 40 kg KT-1PS2 satellite into a 300 km polar orbit, the flight test focused on stage and satellite separation. The KT-1A, originally planned for a 2008 launch, was projected to increase capacity through addition of external strap-on motors. [171]

Development of a follow-on solid launch vehicle centers upon a new 1.7 meter solid rocket motor. The KT-2 is said to be a three or four-stage launch vehicle designed for geosynchronous transfer orbit and polar orbits missions with an estimated payload capability of 300 kg. Plans for a KT-2 were based upon the CASIC Sixth Academy's ability to develop and produce a larger 1.7 m diameter motor, presumably based on the foundation of the SpaB-17 perigee kick motor for communication satellite programs. The KT-2A would add external motors for lifting over 400 kgs into polar orbit. The ultimate requirement appears to be the deployment of a 500 kg payload to a 700 km orbit.[172] The status of these programs is unclear.

Near Space Surveillance Platforms

Beyond traditional space-based platforms, development of "near space" sensors appears to have a relatively high priority. Coverage from platforms similar to satellites in low earth orbit could offer significant improvements in resolution. Duration of flight for near space vehicles far exceeds that of unmanned aerial vehicles (UAVs) and their small radar and thermal cross-sections make them difficult to track and target. Powered in part by high efficiency solar cells, near space vehicles are viewed as a relatively inexpensive means of persistent broad area surveillance.[173] Over the coming decade, near space flight vehicles may emerge as an important platform for a persistent regional surveillance capability during crisis situations.[174]

While technical challenges exist, the PLA and China's defense R&D community have become increasingly interested in near space flight vehicles for reconnaissance, communications relay, electronic countermeasures.[175] SAR surveillance and electronic intelligence appear to be priorities.[176] In order to overcome technical challenges, CASIC established a new research institute in 2005 dedicated to the design, development, and manufacturing of near space flight vehicles for surveillance purposes. Known as the 068 Base Near Space Flight Vehicle R&D Center and located in Hunan province, its initial projects include the JK-5, JK-12, and JKZ -20 airships. 068 Base has a cooperative R&D program with Russian counterparts for upper atmospheric airship control systems.[177]

In summary, military and civilian authorities are leveraging the talent that exists within the space industry to field a wide range of increasingly advanced space capabilities. China is gradually improving in its ability to overcome complex systems engineering challenges and field reliable and cost effective space systems. National level space programs are examples of progress that is being made. Other programs, including space-based sensors, communications systems, operationally responsive microsatellites, and near space platforms support a PLA that is able to conduct an increasingly diverse range of military operations.

SECTION 5:

SPACE SUPPORT FOR PLA INTEGRATED JOINT OPERATIONS

Senior PRC civilian leaders within the party and government view space as a national priority and direct significant resources toward the country's space-related R&D and technology base. Effective utilization of the space domain, and ability to deny others the use of space, is also central to PRC defense modernization goals. The operational demands of "informatized" warfare and integrated joint operations, or the ability of individual services to coordinate operations, drive investment into space technologies. Space systems enable long-range precision strike operations during campaigns to enforce territorial claims and resolve sovereignty disputes. Conventional ballistic missiles in particular have been one the most effective tools of PRC political and military coercion, and perhaps the most visible and central element of PRC's coercive strategy against Taiwan.

Space systems, including remote sensing, navigation, communications, weather, and survey and mapping satellites, enable the delivery of conventional payloads at increasingly long distances.[178] An assured ability to penetrate air and missile defenses and neutralize targets with precision strikes enables sustained dominance over the skies of a particular region. The integrated application of space systems; long-range precision assets such as ballistic missiles; and manned air combat platforms; creates synergies that could allow the attainment of air superiority in regional conflicts. Air superiority in turn facilitates freedom of action on the ground and on the seas. Increasingly accurate and lethal ballistic and land attack cruise missiles are a means to suppress air defenses and air operations even with relatively backward air forces.

Looking horizontally beyond its immediate periphery and vertically into space, Chinese analysts view disruption of the U.S. ability to project conventional power as a legitimate force modernization goal. The ability to operate freely in space and deny others freedom of operation facilitates defense against advanced U.S. long-range precision strike capabilities expected to be in place by 2025.[179] Promoting the merging of air and space into a single integrated aerospace domain, Chinese writings stress the importance of space technology in a broader "national aerospace security system."[180] Space systems also help reduce vulnerability to first strikes against China's nuclear deterrent, and help assure the ability to carry out a retaliatory response.

Finally, more efficient and effective systems for leveraging military-related technologies are shaping new operational and organizational concepts that best accommodate new capabilities, such as long-range precision strike and counter-space systems. Over the next 10-15 years, the PLA is expected to expand its integrated architecture of sensors, communications, long-range precision strike assets, and other joint operational capabilities. As it proceeds, the

PLA may have greater confidence in its ability to enforce a broader range of territorial claims around China's periphery.

Role of the General Staff Department in Space Operations

The General Staff Department oversees a broad and diffuse organizational infrastructure for developing requirements and operating portions of the ground segment supporting space operations. Entities within GSD, the Air Force, the Navy, and the Second Artillery appear to play a key role in developing operational requirements for surveillance and other space systems applications. GSD, GAD, and Service missions could evolve as Chinese competencies in space expand. While previous studies have addressed GSD organizational issues, the process for how GSD develops operational requirements remains opaque.[181]

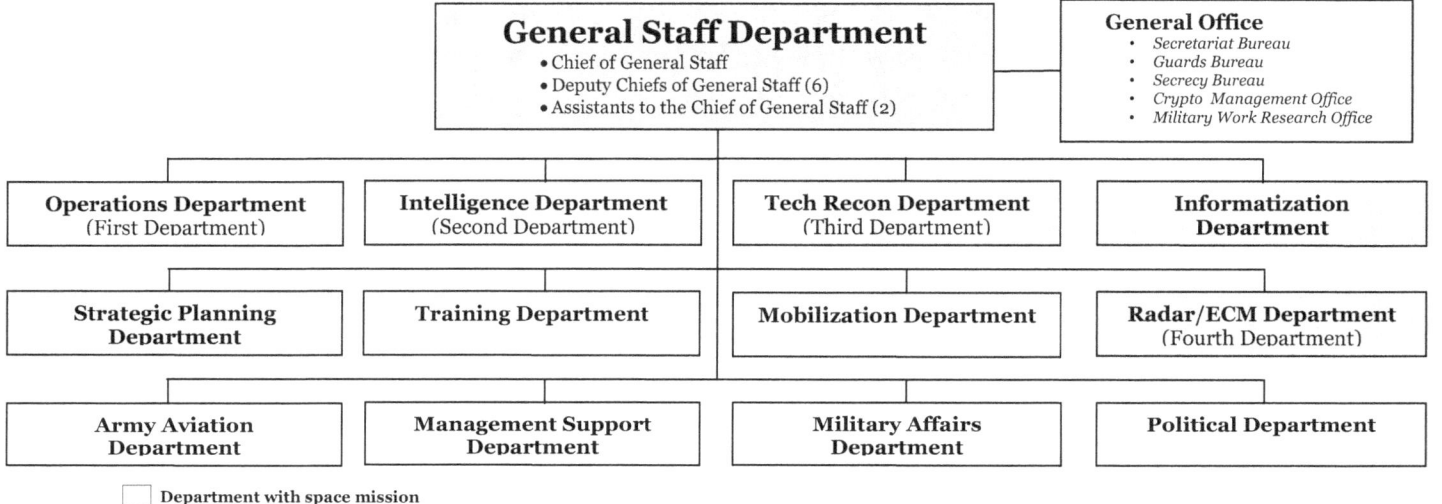

First Department (Operations Department)

The GSD Operations Department develops requirements for and manages joint military use of navigation, geodetic, metrological, and oceanographic space systems. The Survey and Mapping Bureau manages the ground segment of the Beidou satellite positioning system.[182] The bureau leverages a national satellite laser ranging (SLR) network for precise determination of satellites, a capability critical for ensuring precision of the Beidou navigation satellite system.[183] The Survey and Mapping Bureau also is believed to operate a very long baseline interferometer (VLBI) network of radio telescopes that support China's space tracking system.[184] The First Department's Weather and Hydrological Bureau manages military meteorological satellite data and also oversees a specialized unit responsible for space weather analysis and forecasting.[185]

Second Department (Intelligence Department)

The GSD Second Department appears to play a role in the development of space-based reconnaissance operational requirements and operation of ground receiving stations. More specifically, the key organization is the GSD Second Department Technology Bureau, also known as the Beijing Institute of Remote Sensing Information or GSD Space Technology Reconnaissance Bureau. Based in the northern Beijing suburb of Qinghe, the GSD Space Reconnaissance Bureau appears to be primarily focused on electro-optical (EO) and synthetic aperture radar (SAR) remote sensing operations.[186]

Third Department (Technical Reconnaissance Department)

The GSD Third Department functions as China's primary signals intelligence (SIGINT) collection and analysis entity. Headquartered in the Xianghongqi area of Xishan and organized into 12 regional and functional bureaus, the GSD Third Department manages a large bureaucracy for communications intelligence (COMINT) collection, translation, and analysis. Headquartered in Shanghai's Zhabei District, the 12th Bureau intercepts satellite communications from sites throughout China and possibly from space-based collection assets.[187] It appears to maintain a close linkage with the GSD Second Department's Beijing Institute of Remote Sensing Information.[188] Subordinate offices under the Twelfth Bureau operate satellite monitoring facilities in Changchun (Jilin Province), Fuzhou and Xiamen (Fujian Province), Hangzhou (Zhejiang Province), Guangzhou (Guangdong Province), Kunming (Yunnan Province), and in Xinjiang.[189]

Informatization Department

The GSD Informatization Department (formerly the Communications Department) develops operational requirements for and oversees use of dedicated military communications satellites, such as the Fenghuo and Shentong systems (ChinaSat-22 and ChinaSat-20). Key organizations within the Informatization Department responsible for developing operational and technical requirements include the Equipment Bureau and S&T Bureau 61st Research Institute.

Strategic Planning Department

A relatively new organization – the GSD Strategic Planning Department – may support the Chief of General Staff in conducting term analysis of the international security environment, including space-related trends. The Strategic Planning Department also appears responsible for organizational transformation, strategic resource allocation, and departmental and "domain" coordination (e.g., between GSD and GAD). Although speculative, the department may play a central role in force planning for future space operations.[190]

Fourth Department (Radar and Electronic Countermeasures Department)

The GSD Fourth Department is responsible for radar and electronic countermeasures and appears capable of disrupting adversary use of communications, navigation, synthetic aperture radar and other satellites. The Fourth Department may oversee one or possibly two satellite jamming regiments.[191] The Fourth Department may operate electronic reconnaissance satellite ground receiving stations to support joint targeting. The PLA Electronic Engineering Academy is the Fourth Department's institution for professional military education and technical training.[192]

PLA Counterspace Development

Freedom of action in space, and an ability to deny an adversary access to its space assets, offer military advantages in land, air, maritime, and information domains.[193] The United States and other powers are dependent on space assets for military operations and to ensure an advantage over potential adversaries. The U.S. relies on space-based assets for communications, navigation, missile warning, environmental monitoring, and reconnaissance. Given vulnerabilities in space infrastructure, a potential adversary could target U.S. space capabilities and seek to deny advantages gained through the leveraging of space capabilities. Space superiority is characterized by the freedom to operate in space while denying the same to an adversary.[194]

The PRC has been investing in a range of passive and active counterspace technologies, and has a demonstrated a rudimentary capability to track and intercept satellites orbiting around the earth's poles in the lower reaches of outer space.[195] Chinese pundits highlight trends toward militarization of space and outline requirements for counterspace operations in future conflicts. However, non-destructive means of denying an enemy use of satellites and mitigating threats from space debris may be a more urgent priority than fielding kinetic kill vehicles. As noted by former Director, National Intelligence ADM (ret) Dennis Blair, "counter-command, control, and sensor systems, to include communications satellite jammers, are among Beijing's highest military priorities."[196] China also is investing into the means to deny an adversary effective use of space surveillance assets through concealment, camouflage, and deception.[197] Elements of a viable counterspace program include an architecture that fuses multiple sources of data in order to detect, identify, and track satellites and other space objects; development and production of technologies that neutralize threats; and a clearly defined and well trained organization able to coordinate and execute counterspace operations.

Space Surveillance Network

Counterspace operations depend upon a survivable space surveillance network, and China is gradually developing a supporting infrastructure. China's ability to track and mitigate space debris could serve as a metric for the amount of progress that is being made. In 2003, CNSA initiated a long term action plan (2006-2020) for detecting and mitigating space debris. The program includes a planned space-based surveillance system for tracking debris, satellites, and other objects in space.[198]

The CAS Space Target and Debris Observation and Research Center provides early warning of small debris threatening manned orbital vehicles, a role that was highlighted during the Shenzhou-7 mission. In October 2009, Chinese media reporting described the nation's first satellite maneuver to avoid a collision. The satellite may have been one of the Yaogan series.[199] Possibly linked with the CAS surveillance network, GAD facilities for space debris surveillance were completed in Yao'an County, north of the Yunnan Province city of Chuxiong.[200] The PLA and civilian counterparts also have been enhancing national satellite laser range finding capabilities, and investing in radar systems for satellite surveillance and tracking.[201]

Kinetic Kill Vehicle Development

China has demonstrated an ability to engage targets in space as part of a broader effort to field a "national aerospace security system."[202] Chinese writings tend to link counterspace with an ability to track and engage all flight vehicles transiting space, including ballistic missiles.[203] China's counterspace program appears to parallel interest in countermeasures against advanced U.S. long-range precision strike capabilities that would transit space, and are expected to be in place by 2025.[204] Among these include the Force Application and Launch from the Continental U.S. (FALCON) Hypersonic Technology Vehicle (HTV) program, U.S. Air Force X-37B Orbital Test Vehicle first boosted into space in April 2010 and the X-51A, which would be dropped from a B-52 and boosted to hypersonic speeds by a rocket before its experimental scramjet engine is initiated.[205]

China's space and missile industry conducted successful tests of a KKV in January 2007 and January 2010, thus demonstrating an ability to intercept polar orbiting satellites and rudimentary medium range ballistic missiles during the mid-course of flight. The ASAT test coincided with legislative debates on Taiwan regarding investment of resources into satellite systems and an associated launch vehicle.[206] At least one KKV funding source during the late 1990s and earlier this decade appears to be the 863-409 program (and possibly the 863-706 program).[207] Presumably these technologies (some common with the PLA ASBM program) include active millimeter wave and possible passive imaging infra-red (IIR) terminal guidance, and automated target recognition (ATR) software. Among the research entities involved during initial KKV R&D - euphemistically referred to as a space interceptor - was the Harbin Institute of Technology.[208]

Counterspace Organization

The lead organization within the PLA for counterspace operations remains an open question, as does the relationship between national space and counterspace policies and programs. GAD-affiliated organizations have produced assessments of space strategy, characterizing space power and advocating the prioritization of space technology in order to further PLA warfighting under conditions of "informatization," including counterspace operations and "space superiority." Analysts differentiate between "hard" and "soft" counterspace measures, and the potential relevance of an independent "space force" that would centralize space operations under a unified command.[209]

Discussion of an independent space force has been underway since the 1990s, and resolution of the issue has yet to clear. The GAD Headquarters Department (CLTC) oversees China's three main launch centers and satellite tracking and control network. There have been discussions within the PLA leadership on splitting off CLTC into an independent space command, or placing the counterspace mission under control of the PLAAF or Second Artillery, but there has been no concrete evidence of subordination to date. GSD appears to retain control over the "take" from reconnaissance satellites. However, which of these entities might develop operational requirements; exercise oversight over R&D; and carry out the "space defense" mission (to include anti-satellite and missile defense) has yet to be determined.

Regardless, both the PLAAF and Second Artillery have indicated intent to establish space operations as a core competency. The PLAAF argues that battlespace for air defense operations should be extended beyond the atmosphere and into space and over sea, yet integrated under a single air defense command organization.[210] Under an ambitious and long term force development concept of "integrated air and space (aerospace) operations," the PLAAF is the leading candidate to serve as the country's principle custodian of an evolving aerospace defense system.[211] As PLAAF Commander Xu Qiliang argued in a 2009 media interview, an integrated approach to aerospace operations is needed to ensure strategic dominance on the sea and ground.[212] PLAAF-affiliated analysts have outlined the service's intent to "leapfrog" in its ability to conduct integrated aerospace operations.[213] With the concept of counterspace operations still in its infancy, observers note that technological and legal issues constrain the pace of development.[214] Nevertheless, as one senior PLAAF official noted, "space control is a reasonable extension of air control."[215]

Meanwhile, the Second Artillery has argued that it should be responsible for military space operations. For example, an internal Second Artillery text references a "Second Artillery space operations unit" as an operational support function.[216] However, no clear operational infrastructure for a space mission is evident in Second Artillery order of battle. Theoretically, existing medium, intermediate, and intercontinental ballistic missiles could be adapted for a space intercept role by reprogramming missile guidance and fusing.[217]

One analysis explains that the aerospace defense domain would be divided along the Karman Line: the PLAAF would assume the air defense mission for threats below 100 km, while the Second Artillery would be responsible for threats above 100 km.[218] A senior PLAAF Equipment Department authority noted the service's investment into missile defense development.[219]

Regardless, uncertainty surrounds the role of the GAD, PLAAF, Second Artillery, or other entities in managing space operations, including planning, programming, and budgeting functions; satellite launch, tracking, and control; ground processing; and counter-space operations. Another potentially contentious issue could be ownership over future flight vehicles that operate in or transit all domains of space, near space, and the terrestrial atmosphere.[220]

As a final note, the United States, Japan, and the United Kingdom among others have cited concerns over the implications of China's ASAT test and other counterspace programs for the potential militarization of space. Beijing has responded by reinforcing its own positions regarding the need to safeguard the peaceful use of outer space and preventing the weaponization of outer space. The PRC has acceded to a number of international space treaties, including the Outer Space Treaty, and has defended its actions as being consistent with international law.

Space Support for Long-Range Precision Strike

China's space program is intimately connected with the country's ballistic missile programs. In addition to common technologies, synergies are created through integration of space, air, and long-range precision strike operations that exemplify the PLA's evolving concept of air and space (aerospace) power. Aerospace power is the key to gaining strategic advantages by application of military force via platforms operating in or passing through air and space.

Since the inception of China's space program, launch vehicles have had dual-use applications for transport of satellites into orbit and delivery of nuclear payloads to targets within the region and around the world. With the introduction of dedicated conventional long-range precision strike systems, the direct linkage has weakened. Regardless, long-range precision strike systems, such as the CASC First Academy's DF-15 SRBM, have long been the centerpiece of China's coercive military strategy directed against Taiwan. China's R&D community appears to be examining prospects for expanding the range of its conventional strike capability, to include developing capabilities for prompt global strike operations similar to those conducted by the U.S. military. Based on a broad survey of available literature, a phased approach could lead toward a conventional global strike capability by 2025. The initial phase appears to involve a rudimentary capability to strike stationary and mobile targets on land and at sea out to a range of up to 2,000 km by the conclusion of the 11th Five Year (2006-2010). Indications exist that the Second Artillery introduced its first anti-ship ballistic missiles into the active inventory before the end of 2010.

A second phase would seek to extend these capabilities out to a range of 3,000 km by the conclusion of the 12th Five Year Plan (2011-2015). The options include a more advanced solid motor and an adjusted trajectory in which the ballistic missile's delivery vehicle remains within the atmosphere. China's R&D community appears to be investing in a new generation of aerospace flight vehicles that blur the distinction between the air and space domains. In discussing new generation ballistic and extended range air and ground launched cruise missiles, aerospace engineers have advocated modification of existing ballistic missile designs toward ones that adopt characteristics of both ballistic and cruise missiles. As two aerospace engineers put it:

"The traditional ballistic reentry mode of reentry vehicle cannot meet the demand of the new battle environment. A new-style lift reentry weapon platform is an optimal key to solve this problem."[221]

CASC First Academy's first two-staged conventional ballistic missile recently completed conceptual design flight tests. Existing SRBMs have a single solid rocket motor. The CASC First Academy missile system is said to remain in the atmosphere the entire range of its flight.[222] A system on a depressed ballistic trajectory with a maneuverable post-boost vehicle likely would complicate detection and engagement by sea-based missile defense interceptors, such as the Standard Missile-3 (SM-3).

A third phase would focus on extending a conventional precision strike capability out to 8,000 km before the end of the 13th Five Year Plan in 2020, and a global precision strike capability by the end of the 14th Five Year Plan in 2025.[223] Should such a scenario unfold, U.S. and Chinese long-range precision strike assets would hold at risk any unhardened facility on earth with conventional munitions. A proven guidance, navigation, and control package capable of acquiring and engaging maritime targets could be integrated with an extended range ballistic missile, assuming that speed can be controlled and space-based sensors are available to support targeting at longer ranges.[224]

Hypersonic aerospace flight vehicles exemplify the merging of the air and space domains from both an operational and industrial perspective.[225] Aerospace strike systems under development in China could be divided into two categories: 1) a boost-glide vehicle that is launched into a sub-orbital trajectory in near space by a ballistic missile; or 2) a horizontal take off and landing strike system that utilizes an airbreathing supersonic combustion ramjet (scramjet) engine to propel a vehicle to hypersonic speeds. Key areas of R&D include high lift-to-drag ratio delivery vehicles, high temperature materials for thermal protection, precision navigation, guidance and control, and ability to maintain external radiofrequency links through plasma in near space.[226]

An initial transatmospheric vehicle design is believed to rely on conventional ballistic missile technology for ascent into a sub-orbital trajectory in near space.[227] The missile would then release a post-boost vehicle to glide and maneuver toward the intended target. Chinese engineers appear to be conducting preliminary research into a conceptual design for a suborbital flight vehicle or strike system that adopts a boost-glide trajectory.[228] Instead of flying on a normal ballistic path that takes the missile into space before returning to earth, the boost-glide missile skips in and out of near space, those altitudes between 20 and 100 km.[229]

Aerodynamically configured to glide toward its target, the flight vehicle adopts hybrid characteristics of both ballistic and cruise missiles. In its initial stage of flight, sources indicate the flight vehicle would reach hypersonic speeds of between Mach 8 and Mach 12.[230] Another study references an upper altitude of 60 km and lower of 30 km.[231] In addition to complicating mid-course missile defenses, boost glide flight vehicles are said to extend the range of existing ballistic missiles. One study, for example, asserts that a basic boost-glide capability would extend the range of a missile by 31.2%.[232]

Chinese long-range precision strike capabilities would also benefit from improvements in SAR capabilities. China's aerospace industry appears to be investing significant resources into fielding a missile-borne SAR capability that would be integrated with satellite positioning and inertial navigation systems.[233] Intimately connected to China's air- and space-based SAR programs, the advantages of missile-borne SAR include all-weather capability, high resolution, extended range imaging, and autonomous guidance. During flight, a SAR seeker could penetrate cloud cover to acquire a maritime surface target, and then relinquish targeting guidance to another active or passive seeker in the terminal flight phase. An on-board SAR system would be activated after slowing the missile down to below hypersonic speeds (e.g., below Mach 5 depending on various factors).[234] A number of technical studies also discuss an integrated high altitude and low altitude guidance system.[235] Chinese engineers highlight the need for a highly accurate and high speed inertial measurement unit to compensate for the motion of the missile and the quality of SAR components. Engineers also have developed electronic warfare simulations to ensure the survivability of on-board SAR systems.[236] In terms of cost, technical commentators have noted that a radar package may be the most expensive aspect of an extended range precision strike program. [237]

The PLA's extended range conventional strike capability also includes ground and air-launched land attack cruise missiles. Since successful completion of operational testing in October 2003, the PLA's inventory of ground launched cruise missiles has expanded significantly. The addition of air-launched land attack cruise missiles will further expand the PLA's extended range strike capability.[238] At least one cruise missile designer has highlighted six focus areas for next generation weapon systems, including 1) increased range; 2) increased precision, 3) higher reliability, 4) increased weapon system effects, 5) easier maintenance, and 6) improved ECCM.[239] Such weapons rely upon space-based remote sensing and navigation systems.

In summary, the PLA is improving its ability to monitor events in the Asia-Pacific region through an expanded system of space-based remote sensing, communications, and navigation satellites. As its persistent sensor and command and control architecture increases in sophistication and range, the PLA's ability to hold at risk an expanding number of targets throughout the western Pacific Ocean, South China Sea, and elsewhere around its periphery is expected to grow. Second Artillery and PLAAF force modernization appears to be focused on systems able to suppress air operations on Guam, throughout the South China Sea, and other locations by 2015.[240] Increasingly accurate conventional ballistic and GLCMs are the optimal means for suppressing enemy air defense and creating a more permissive environment for subsequent conventional air operations due to their relative immunity to defense systems.

CONCLUSION

The PRC has made significant advances in its space program and is emerging as a space power. In addition to bolstering the political prestige of the CCP, advances in space will enable more effective military operations at increasingly greater distances from Chinese shores. Over the next 10-15 years, more advanced precision strike assets, integrated with persistent space-based surveillance, a single integrated air and space picture, and survivable communications architecture, could enhance greater confidence in enforcing a broader range of territorial claims around China's periphery.

The PLA oversees a broad and diffuse organizational infrastructure for developing requirements and overseeing R&D, manufacturing, and operation of space systems. As access to foreign technology grows, bridges between various bureaucracies established through initiatives such as the 863 Program appear to facilitate more efficient diffusion of technology within China's civilian and military sectors. The overlap between civilian and military applications of space technology is considerable, and it is often difficult to draw a clear line of separation between them.

Aerospace power has been one of the most effective tools of PRC political and military coercion. Although other interests compete for attention and resources, the Taiwan scenario remains the principle strategic direction of PRC national security policy makers, defense planners, and acquisition authorities. Taiwan is a core interest of the United States. As such, the United States should maintain the capacity to resist any resort to force or other forms of coercion that would jeopardize the security, or the social or economic system, of the people on Taiwan. Barring a PRC renunciation of the use of force to resolve political differences with Taiwan and a significant reduction in the PLA military posture directed against island, space cooperation likely will remain limited.

While the overall level of its space technology may not match that of the United States and other space faring nations, China's relative advances are significant. Given asymmetries in reliance on space systems, even relative increases in Chinese space capabilities could present challenges for the United States. A survivable space-based sensor architecture, able to transmit reconnaissance data to ground sites in China in near-real time, facilitates the PLA's ability to project firepower at greater distances and with growing lethality and speed. Trends indicate that China's basic satellite coverage of waters and land within the Asia-Pacific region could, over time, approach that of the United States. The range of China's precision strike assets is expanding out to Guam, Australia, Southeast Asia, and India. Space assets could provide deployed ASBM assets under the Second Artillery with highly accurate geo-locational data on intervening US forces.

China also is pressing forward with an ambitious counterspace program, including a ground- and space-based space surveillance systems, electronic warfare capabilities, and KKVs.

A space surveillance system capable of detecting and tracking objects with low radar cross sections is a fundamental prerequisite for effective and precise counterspace operations. The PLA service assigned the operational counterspace mission remains an open question.

Space technology also will continue to be an important driver for economic growth. Satellite sales and launch services offer China's defense industrial complex with an augmenting source of revenue. Technology spin offs may offer competitive advantages in certain sectors, such as satellite navigation products. Exports of space technology sales pose challenges to the United States not only because of China's non-market based economy, but also because of military and security concerns.[241]

China's interaction with other space faring powers furthers national political, scientific, technological, and economic goals. Space is a significant metric of national power, and the United States remains a world leader within this domain. However, China is emerging as a relative competitor in selected areas of space technology. While collaboration in space may benefit both the United States and China, Beijing's lack of transparency over military budgets, and potential risks associated with the military applications of space technology, remain major causes for concern.

APPENDIX 1:

INTERNATIONAL SPACE COOPERATION

Since the beginning of its space program in the 1950s, the PRC has prioritized international space-related interactions in order to further national political, scientific, technological, and economic goals. Focusing on space-related S&T, as well as the application of space systems, China National Space Administration (CNSA) has formed multilateral and bilateral partnerships with a wide range of international partners.[242]

Former Soviet Union. PRC aerospace interaction with the former Soviet Union has a 50 year history. In 1957, Qian Xuesen led a military delegation to Moscow to lay the foundation for a Sino-Russian technical relationship. The relationship involved hundreds of Soviet engineers working in Chinese research institutes, Chinese students studying in the Union of Soviet Socialist Republics (USSR), and the transfer of technical designs to China. The Soviets and the Chinese were engaged in 343 contracts and 257 technical projects, including some in the aerospace realm. In August 1960, however, the relationship was abruptly ended due to the Sino-Soviet split.

A cooperative framework with Russian space counterparts was established in 1991, and has continued through the present day. Representatives from Chinese and Soviet space industries signed an initial agreement in Moscow in May 1990 on 10 cooperative projects, the first of which addressed joint efforts to develop a GLONASS/GPS compatible receiver. A formal contract was signed 2 years later. The relationship was solidified when, on December 18, 1992, CASC and the Russian Space Agency signed an official protocol for the sharing of space technology. This agreement was formalized during President Yeltsin's visit to Beijing where he also signed a no-first-use pledge with the Chinese. A follow-on agreement, signed by CASC and the head of the Russian Space Agency, outlined at least 10 areas of space cooperation including exchanges in satellite navigation, space surveillance, propulsion, satellite communications, joint design efforts, materials, intelligence sharing, scientific personnel exchanges, and space systems testing. For program management, the two sides agreed to annual meetings to review the various cooperative programs.

Space cooperation was formalized at the working group level within the framework of regular Prime Minister-level meetings in 2000. Cooperation is spread across almost 50 areas, including lunar and Mars exploration.[243] In 2006, the Russian Federal Space Agency announced that China and Russia were cooperating on lunar exploration and had plans to reach a "joint lunar exploration agreement by the end of the year."[244] Based on an agreement signed in 2007, the two sides also are cooperating on a Mars exploration project, centered on the Yinghuo-1 space probe that is scheduled for launch in 2011. In July 2009, CASC Director Ma Xingrui, leaders of CASC departments, and representatives from CGWIC met with counterparts from the Russian Space Agency for further steps to deepen and broaden Sino-

Russian cooperation.[245] The two sides met again in November 2010 to define initiatives for the next two years, and Chinese representatives visited various facilities in Russia.[246] Russia and CASIC's 068 Base signed an agreement in December 2010 for development of near space vehicles.[247] However, the relationship has not always been smooth: In 2007, Russian TsNIIMASH executives were convicted of illegal transfer of aerodynamic modeling data as part of an agreement with CPMIEC.[248]

In addition, Beijing has been expanding its relations with other former Soviet republics. Based on the precedent established with Russia, initial space cooperation agreements were concluded with Ukraine (March 1994), Belarus (June 1994), and Kazakhstan (May 1998). Areas of early cooperation with Ukraine included remote sensing, satellite communications, and aerospace material research and development. More recently, Ukraine's National Space Agency Director Yuriy Alekseyev and China's National Space Administration Director Chen Qiufa signed an agreement in September 2010 covering 50 space programs between 2011 and 2015 in areas such as space-based remote sensing, an ionospheric satellite for forecasting earthquakes, and a range of other initiatives.[249] Space cooperation figured prominently during meetings between Chinese President Hu Jintao and Ukrainian President Viktor Yanukovych in June 2011.[250]

China's National Space Administration and CASC also strengthened relations with counterparts in Kazhakstan (KazCosmos). In late 1999, China and Kazakhstan signed a joint communiqué that officially ended the border disputes between the two countries, and cleared ways for further space and other forms of cooperation.[251] Cooperation is said to include remote sensing and scientific satellites, space-based earthquake monitoring, and ionospheric research.[252]

Europe. China has not limited its international cooperation to the former Soviet Union. Building upon a foundation established in the 1980s, contacts between the French and Chinese space communities were initiated during the June 1994 space industry negotiations between France's National Center for Space Studies (CNES) and COSTIND and CASC. Specific areas of discussion included small launch vehicle technology and R&D of small satellites. Two follow-up meetings were held in September 1994 and November 1995. Since 1994, at least 10 Chinese space delegations have visited French space industry facilities. Besides small launch vehicle and satellite technology, cooperation has focused on GPS/GLONASS exploitation, small satellite bus development, satellite attitude control systems, communication satellites, and meteorological satellite technology. The 10th space cooperation meeting was held in Beijing in April 2011.[253]

The space relationship between China and Germany began in the early 1980s, culminating in a contract between the CASC and DaimlerChrysler Aerospace AG (DASA) in 1987 on the DFH-3. A follow-up agreement between CASC and Deutsche Aerospace AG was signed in November 1993, which included the establishment of a joint venture between EuraSpace and CASC called Sinosat. Sinosat's first satellite was Nahuel, a communications satellite scheduled for launch in 1997. Other areas of cooperation include SATCOM transponder technology, solar panels, and orbital control systems. Chinese scientists sought cooperation with German counterparts on a two ton solar telescope that would orbit around the moon about 2002. While unconfirmed, it appears that this cooperative project has been placed on hold.[254]

Cooperation with the European Space Agency includes the Cluster and Double Star programs that have focused on the magnetosphere and effects of the Sun on Earth's environment. The TC-1 (equatorial) and TC-2 (polar) satellites, involving European sensor packages deployed on Chinese buses, were launched in 2003.[255]

Latin America/Africa. Based on successes with the Sino-Brazilian Earth Resources Satellite (CBERS) program (launches in 1999 and 2003), China has been expanding its space cooperation with other Latin American and African countries. CGWIC concluded a contract with Venezuela in 2005 for the production and launch of a communications satellite, the initial customer in the region for a Chinese manufactured satellite. The satellite entered service in 2009. Venezuelan officials signed a subsequent agreement with CGWIC in May 2011 to provide launch services for the Venezuela Remote-Sensing Satellite 1 Project (VRSS-1) on an LM-4B from Jiuquan Space Launch Center. The satellite was developed by CAST. China is manufacturing and launching a communications satellite for Bolivia, based on its DFH-4 satellite bus. The satellite is scheduled for launch in 2013 on an LM-3B from Xichang.[256] CGWIC also contracted with the Nigerian government for production and launch of a DFH-4 communications satellite.[257]

Southeast Asia. In addition to satellite launch services for a Laotian program, China has also been examining cooperative efforts with Indonesia.[258] The Laotian government contracted with CGWIC for the sale and launch of a DFH platform for broadcast and communications. The launch vehicle is the LM-3B.[259] An agreement has also been concluded with Thailand for a satellite remote sensing ground station.[260]

U.S.-China Space Interaction. U.S.-PRC ambitions in space have experienced a turbulent relationship between civilian and military actors in both countries. Sanctions imposed after the Tiananmen Massacre in 1989 imposed limits on the transfer of technology to the PRC, including in the aerospace arena. Prior to 1999, bilateral cooperation in space was largely limited to export licensing of U.S. satellites, which generated as much as $1 billion in revenue for U.S. aerospace firms. The Office of the U.S. Trade Representative (USTR) negotiated an initial agreement in 1988 intended to safeguard U.S. technology when granting export licenses to U.S. industry for sales of U.S. satellites to Chinese customers. Separate agreements regulated the number of U.S. satellites to be launched on Chinese launch vehicles.

Since 1999, U.S. satellites have been subject to restrictions under International Traffic in Arms Regulations (ITAR) due to export control concerns, effectively barring any use of Chinese launch vehicles.[261] Although authorities in Beijing have highlighted the need for bilateral collaboration and information sharing, U.S. uncertainty over the motives and goals of the Chinese space program – and the successful PRC destruction of a decommissioned weather satellite in January 2007 – have been limiting factors. Subsequent economic, political, and security tensions between the United States and China have largely halted space cooperation.[262]

Government-to-government interactions on space issues were renewed in 2006 when NASA Administrator Michael Griffin visited Beijing.[263] They received further boosts under President Obama, as space cooperation was mentioned in both Joint Statements issued after the two Hu-Obama summits, as well as NASA Administrator Charles Bolden's visit in October 2010. Recently, however, Congressional action halted almost all interaction between NASA and Chinese space entities. Language in Fiscal Year 2011 appropriations legislation restricts NASA and White House Office of Science and Technology Policy from "develop[ing], design[ing], plan[ning], promulgat[ing], implement[ing], or execut[ing] a bilateral policy, program, order, or contract of any kind to participate, collaborate, or coordinate bilaterally in any way with China or any Chinese-owned company," and banned all official Chinese visitors at any NASA facilities.[264]

Areas of cooperation that have been raised include information and data sharing, analysis of environmental and meteorological data, agreements on space policy and protocol, and joint space exercises. Disadvantages to space cooperation with China include inadvertent sensitive technology transfer, moral questions surrounding granting legitimacy to an authoritarian party-state with a poor human rights record, and the PRC's continued reliance on military coercion to resolve political disputes with Taiwan and other neighbors in the region.[265] A detailed assessment of technology transfer risks associated with space cooperation, the sale of commercial satellites, or the launch of U.S. satellites on Chinese launch vehicles, remains unavailable.

ENDNOTES

[1] For examples of U.S. overviews of China's space modernization, see Dean Cheng, "Prospects for China's Military Space Efforts," in Roy Kamphausen, David Lai , and Andrew Scobell (eds), *Beyond The Strait: PLA Missions Other Than Taiwan* (Carlisle PA: 2009), pp. 211-252, at http://www.strategicstudiesinstitute.army.mil/pdffiles/pub910.pdf; Gregory Kulacki, "A Space Race with China," *Harvard Asia Pacific*, pp. 12-15.Eric Hagt and Matthew Durnin, "China's Antiship Ballistic Missile: Developments and Missing Links," *Naval War College Review* 62, no. 4 (Autumn 2009), pp. 87–115; Andrew S. Erickson, "Eyes in the Sky," *U.S. Naval Institute Proceedings*, Vol. 136, No. 4 (April 2010), pp. 36-41; Gregory Kulacki and Jeffrey G. Lewis, *A Place for One's Mat: China's Space Program, 1956–2003* (Cambridge, MA: American Academy of Arts and Sciences, 2009), at http://www.amacad.org/publications/spaceChina.pdf; Kevin Pollpeter, "The Chinese Vision of Space Military Operations," pp, 329-369, in *China's Revolution in Doctrinal Affairs: Emerging Trends in the Operational Art of the Chinese People's Liberation Army*, edited by James Mulvenon and David Finklestein, CNA Corporation, Virginia. December 2005, at http://www.defensegroupinc.com/cira/pdf/doctrinebook_ch9.pdf; Larry M. Wortzel, *The Chinese People's Liberation Army and Space Warfare: Emerging United States-China Military Competition* (Wash DC: American Enterprise Institute, 2007), at http://www.aei.org/paper/26977; Michael P. Pillsbury, "An Assessment of China's Anti-Satellite and Space Warfare Programs, Policies , and Doctrines," Report for the U.S.-China Economic and Security Review Commission, January 19, 2007, at http://www.uscc.gov/researchpapers/2007/FINAL_REPORT_1-19-2007_REVISED_BY_MPP.pdf; Alanna Krolikowski, "China's Civil and Commercial Space Activities and their Implications," Testimony before the U.S.-China Economic and Security Review Commission Hearing on the "Implications of China's Military and Civil Space Programs, May 11, 2011, at http://www.gwu.edu/~spi/assets/docs/11_05_11_krolikowski_testimony.pdf; Dean Cheng "China's Space Program: Civilian, Commercial, and Military Aspects," CNA Corporation Conference Report, May 2006; Phillip C. Saunders, "China's Future in Space: Implications for U.S. Security," *AdAstra*, Spring 2005, pp. 21-23, at http://www.space.com/adastra/china_implications_0505.html; and Joan Johnson-Freese, China's Space Ambitions, *IFRI Proliferation Paper*, Summer 2007, at www.ifri.org/downloads/China_Space_Johnson_Freese.pdf.

[2] Wayne A. Ulman, "China's Emergent Military Aerospace and Commercial Aviation Capabilities," Testimony before the U.S.- China Economic and Security Review Commission, 20 May 2010, http://www.uscc.gov/hearings/2010hearings/written_testimonies/10_05_20_wrt/10_05_20_ulman_statement.php.

[3] See, for example, Dean Cheng, China's Space Program: A Growing Factor in U.S. Security Planning, *Heritage Backgrounder*, August 16, 2011, at http://www.heritage.org/Research/Reports/2011/08/Chinas-Space-Program-A-Growing-Factor-in-US-Security-Planning.

[4] See "To Guarantee Effective Implementation of the Eleventh Five-Year Plan Measure No.2 – To Adjust and Perfect National Economic Policy" [确保 "十一五" 规划有效实施的举措之二——调整和完善经济政策], The Office of the State Council [国务院办公厅], March 18, 2006, at http://www.gov.cn/node_11140/2006-03/18/content_230061.htm. For the most recent space white paper, see "China's Space Activities in 2011," *China Daily*, December 30, 2011, at http://www.chinadaily.com.cn/cndy/2011-12/30/content_14354558.htm.

[5] For an overview of 863 Program management, see "Measures for the Administration of Special Funds of the National High Technology Research and Development Program (863 Program)" [国家高技术研究发展计划（863计划）专项经费管理办法], Ministry of Science and Technology website,

http://www.863.gov.cn/news/3537.htm. As an example of grants awarded to the academic community, Zhejiang University has been actively involved in two related basic research programs, the 863-801 and 863-805 programs.

[6] Feng Jing,"863 Program Spurs Science and Technology," *Beijing Review*, March 29, 2001. [] Another initiative with possible relevance is the defense portion of the 973 Program (National Security Basic Research;[国家安全重大基础研究]). The 973 Program was launched in 1998,

[7] The 863-4 series of projects are referred to as Advanced Defense (先进防御). Special research topics under each 863 subject area is known as a *zhuanti*. The Precision Guidance Expert Group has been headed by Chen Dingchang, former CASIC Second Academy Director. See "Introduction to Chen Dingchang, at http://www.casic.com.cn/n16/n1250/n10984/n17506/17672.html. Bao Weimin [包□民], director of the CASC First Academy's new 10th Research Institute, serves as deputy. Other key players in this group include Yao Yu [姚郁], head of the Harbin Institute of Technology; Yin Xinliang, former Second Academy Director, CASIC Director, and currently Deputy Chairman of CASIC's S&T Advisory Group; Zhang Tianxu [张天序] an automatic target recognition expert from Huazhong S&T University's Institute for Pattern Recognition and Artificial Intelligence; and Zeng Guangshang [曾广商] from the CASC First Academy's 18th Research Institute. The 863-801 program appears to be aligned with the GAD Precision Guidance Experts Group, with Yao Yu for example serving on both the 863-801 and Precision Guidance Expert Groups. Another expert, Long Teng [龙腾] from Beijing Institute of Technology, also has been on the 863-801 expert group and also sits on the GAD Radar Surveillance Experts Group [总装备部雷达探测专业组] and Satellite Application Expert Group [总装备部卫星应用专业组]. He Songhua [何松华] from Hunan University has been on a number of GAD Committees, with a particular focus on millimeter wave seeker technology, and also was a consultant to the CASIC Second Academy's Second Design Department.

[8] See "National Space Administration Organization and Function," National Space Administration Homepage (undated), at http://www.cnsa.gov.cn/n615709/n620681/n771918/index.html.

[9] For background, see the Committee's website at http://www.ngicc.gov.cn/ziyuan/ziyuan_14.htm.

[10] See Zhou Mingshan, Xu Ming, Li Chengjun, Wu Shiguo, "MMW Passive Countermeasures Technology and the Application of Expanded Graphite" [毫米波无源干扰技术及膨胀石墨在其中的应用], *Journal of Microwaves* (*Weibo xuebao*), 2008 (24)1.

[11] Chen Dingchang, Wan Ziming, Lin Jin, and Liu Decheng, "Review of U.S. SPIE'98 Aerodynamics and Opto-Electronics Conference" [美国SPIE'98气动光学会议介绍及相关技术考察], *Aerospace Technology and Civilian Products* [航天技术与民品], May 1999, at http://www.space.cetin.net.cn/docs/mp9905/mp990513.htm.

[12] For reference to a Ukrainian relationship on resolving heating problems, see the Academy of Sciences website at http://www.ipp.kiev.ua/about/conne_e.htm.

[13] Harlan W. Jencks, "COSTIND Is Dead, Long Live COSTIND! Restructuring China's Defense Scientific, Technical, And Industrial Sector," in James C. Mulvenon and Richard H. Yang (ed.), *The People's Liberation Army in the Information Age* (Santa Monica: RAND Corporation, 2004), pp. 59-77; Evan S. Medeiros, Roger Cliff, Keith Crane, and James C. Mulvenon, *A New Direction for China's Defense Industry* (Santa Monica, CA: Rand Corporation, 2005), at http://www.rand.org/pubs/monographs/2005/RAND_MG334.pdf.

[14] Bao Weimin [包为民], director of the CASC First Academy's new 10th Research Institute (Near Space Flight Vehicle Institute), serves as directors. He is dual-hatted as CASC First Academy S&T Committee Director, and deputy director of the GAD Precision Guidance Experts Group.

[15] The Precision Guidance Expert Group has been headed by Chen Dingchang, former CASIC Second Academy Director. See "Introduction to Comrade Chen Dingchang," China Aerospace Science and Industry Corporation, September 20, 2008 at http://www.casic.com.cn/n16/n1250/n10984/n17506/17672.html. Bao Weimin serves as deputy. The 863-801 program appears to be aligned with the GAD Precision Guidance Experts Group.

[16] Qinghua University professor You Zheng [尤政] leads the GAD MEMS technology expert group. He also served as chief designer for China's Naxing-1 [NS-1] and other microsatellite programs, a cooperative effort between Qinghua University and CASIC First Academy. Weighing just 25kgs, the NS-1 microsatellite was launched in April 2004 and was believed to have served as a major platform for testing of defense-related MEMS systems. See "You Zheng presentation," Qinghua University, June 21, 2010, at http://join-tsinghua.edu.cn/bkzsw/detail.jsp?seq=4003&boardid=35. A key entity within CETC responsible for MEMS is the 13th Research Institute located in Shijiazhuang, Hebei Province. Also known as the Hebei Semiconductor Institute [河北半导体研究所], Zhao Yanjun serves as the 13th Research Institute's Deputy Director and is deputy director of the GAD MEMS technology expert group.

[17] Among its prominent members is Xidian University's Li Jiandong [李建东].

[18] China Electronics Technology Corporation (CETC) Director Wang Zhigang [王志刚] directs this GAD Experts Group.

[19] Director of the GAD Stealth Technology Steering Group is Wu Zhe [武哲]. Born in 1957, Wu is from the Beijing University of Aeronautics and Astronautics (BUAA).

[20] The director of the GAD UAV Technology Expert Working Group is Weng Zhiqian [翁志黔], a professor at the Northwest Polytechnical University in Xian and former visiting scholar at University of Houston. See Northwest Polytechnical University Leadership Overview, at http://www.nwpu.edu.cn/xxgk/ldjj/. In this capacity, Weng Zhiqian and other UAV Technology Expert Working members advise the Central Military Commission and State Council on UAV R&D resource allocation and technology/industry policy.

[21] The Space Equipment Integrated R&D Center [航天装备总体研究发展中心] Senior Engineer is Yang Qiangwen [杨强文].

[22] Among various sources, see "GAD Deputy Director Han Yanlin Inspects Academy Leaders' Work" [总装备部副部长韩延林在我院检查指导工作], Academy of Aerospace Propulsion website, at http://www.aalpt.com/www/newcontents.asp?leaf_id=954. Directors of GAD second-level departments, bases, and the Manned Space Engineering Office are equivalent in grade to a Group Army commander.

[23] The Bureau is directed by Wu Weiqi [吴炜琦], who is a space systems engineer best known for an article published in 2006 outlining a vision for China's future military space architecture. See Wu Weiqi, 'Space Information System Optimization for Long-range Precision Attack" [远程精确打击天基信息支持系统体系优化], *Journal of the Academy Of Equipment Command & Technology*, 2006, 17(3), at www.docin.com/p-57648672.html.

[24] The GAD Beidou Program Office is directed by Ran Chengqi [冉承其]. See "Ran Chengqi: Through Self-Reliant Innovation, Beidou Shines Overhead in Space" [冉承其：自主创新，托举 "北斗" 八星耀太空], Ministry of National Defense website, April 10, 2011, at http://news.mod.gov.cn/tech/2011-04/10/content_4236596.htm. Cai Lanbo [蔡兰波] appears to serve as the GAD Beidou office engineering program manager.

[25] As of April 2011, GAD Chief of Staff is Major General Shang Hong [尚宏]. See "Zhu Fazhong: Energetically Support Mianyang's S&T City Development [朱发忠：大力支持绵阳科技城建设], Lianyungang Information Portal, April 5, 2011, at http://www.lygjiaoyi.com/item-2-18981.html. The GAD Deputy Director most linked with space

programs is Lieutenant General Niu Hongguang. Born in October 1951 and appointed to his current position in July 2009, Niu formerly served as Jiuquan Space Launch Center Chief of Staff and Deputy Commander, and GAD Chief of Staff.

[26] Also see *Chinese Launchers and COMSATs: Development & Commercial Activities*, briefing by Fu Zhiheng (Vice President, China Great Wall Industry Corporation) for World Space Risk Forum, Dubai, February 28-March 1, 2012.

[27] For other references to Shang Hong as CLTC "chairman" and GAD Chief of Staff, see http://211.147.16.26/ztbd/2010zt/20101101/2010110107/201011/t20101103_80818.html; and http://www.cnsa.gov.cn/n1081/n7634/n244209/n244359/260169.html.

[28] "Xichang Satellite Launch Center Can Launch at Least 10 Satellites" [西昌卫星发射中心年发射能力达 10 颗以上], *China Space News*, August 4, 2010. Launch campaigns average 25 days. Also see *Chinese Launchers and COMSATs: Development & Commercial Activities*, briefing by Fu Zhiheng (Vice President, China Great Wall Industry Corporation) for World Space Risk Forum, Dubai, February 28-March 1, 2012.

[29] Craig Covault, "Chinese Test Anti-Satellite Weapon," *Aviation Week & Space Technology*, January 17, 2007, at http://www.aviationweek.com/aw/generic/story_channel.jsp?channel=space&id=news/CHI01177.xml.

[30] Wenchang appears to still carry a designation of the 078 Engineering Command [078工程指挥部]. Some reporting implies an operational subordination to Base 20 at Jiuquan. See [省验收组到我市对有关项目征地移民搬迁安置工作进行初步验收], Wenchang TV.com, November 17, 2011, at http://www.wenchangtv.com/news-show-55483.html. The Wenchang Space Launch Center Director is Major General Wang Weichang [王维昌]. For reference to the LM-5 Tianjin manufacturing facilities, see Xin Dingding, "New Carrier Rocket Series to be Built," *China Daily*, October 31, 2007, at http://www.chinadaily.com.cn/china/2007-10/31/content_6217880.htm.

[31] In years past, the Base 26 network included the 7010 space and missile radar system mounted on the side of Huangyang Mountain in Xuanhua County, north of Beijing. The PLA Air Force originally operated the system when first entering IOC in 1976, but later was resubordinated to Base 26 (old MUCD of 89851 Unit). The system was dismantled in the late 1980s/early 1990s. For an excellent overview of Base 26, see "Loudouzi (The Leaker): Overview of Xian Measurement and Control Center" [漏斗子：西安测控中心概览], Wangchao Network, October 10, 2005, at http://www.1no.net/Article/Print.asp?ArticleID=6279. The author has a record of reliable reporting.

[32] The Xian Satellite Measurement and Control Center, which carries a military cover designator of the 63761 Unit, appears to be a subordinate to the Base 26 command in Weinan. Other subordinate elements are collocated with or near Base 26 general headquarters in the Weinan area; Qingdao (63756 Unit); Xiamen (63758 Unit); Nanning (63760 Unit); Xian (63761 Unit, or Xian P.O. Box 505); Shaxian (Fujian Province) Yangfang Village (63762 Unit);

[33] The commander of 26 Base (63750 Unit) is equivalent in grade to a Group Army commander, or a Second Artillery base. As of May 2011, the 26 Base Commander is Major General Xi Zheng [席政], who formerly directed the Beijing Aerospace Command Center. Base 26 Political Commissar is Liu Jianguo [刘建国].

[34] Although speculative, space tracking data from PLA Air Force radar systems may also may contribute to an single integrated space picture. VLBI sites track space objects simultaneously via telescopes that are combined, emulating a telescope with a size equal to the maximum separation between the telescopes. Using ELINT methodology, VLBI measures the time difference of arrival (TDOA) of radio waves at separate antennas. VLBI sites, presumably subordinate to the brigade or regimental-level 61540 Unit, are in Shanghai Sheshan; Kunming;

Guizhou Qiaodongnan Huangping County; Wulumuqi Nanshan; and Beijing Miyun. See "PLA 61540 Unit Successfully Joins Moon Satellite Tracking and Control" [解放军61540部队成功参与探月卫星测控], China Surveying and Mapping Yearbook [中国测绘年鉴编], July 29, 2008, at http://zgchnj.sbsm.gov.cn/article//ljnjll/lbnj/tz/zdsj/200807/20080700039517.shtml. Other key GSD Surveying Bureau ground stations are located in Hainan. Implying that the lunar program has been at least one driver for the VLBI development and for background on CAS entities involved, see "VLBI Sub-System Integration Meeting for Chang'e-1 Satellite Mission Opens in Shanghai" [嫦娥一号卫星任务VLBI测轨分系统总结会在上海召开], Shanghai Astronomical Observatory website, March 17, 2008, at http://center.shao.ac.cn/plus/view.php?aid=2958.

35 Lu Jie, Wu Li, and Sun Bo, [利用天基雷达观测低地轨道上的危险空间碎片], Remote Sensing Technology and Application, April 2006, pp. 103-108, at http://www.lw23.com/pdf_f45463dc-17f0-4895-b2ac-c9f054db3d58/lunwen.pdf.

36 The center may have an MUCD of the 63999 Unit. See "63999 Unit Job Information," USTC website, November 3, 2004, at http://hbjg.ustc.edu.cn/index.php?Aid=438.

37 For the most comprehensive background on China's ballistic missile program, see John Lewis Wilson and Hua Di, "China's Ballistic Missile Programs: Technologies, Strategies, Goals,". International Security, Vol. 17, No. 2 (Fall 1992).

38 "The LM-2D," China Great Wall Industry Corporation website, April 1, 2010, at http://www.cgwic.com/LaunchServices/LaunchVehicle/LM2D.html.

39 Born in July 1930 and educated in the former Soviet Union, SAST's Sun Jingliang [孙敬良] was Chief Designer of the original LM-4 launch vehicle.
40 "China Aerospace Entities Actively Develop Heavy Solid Launch Vehicle [中国航天部门将积极发展重型固体运载火箭], China Space News, June 12, 2010, at http://news.ifeng.com/mil/2/detail_2010_06/12/1616757_0.shtml; "Gan Xiaosong: 'Forrest Gump's' Run on the Innovation Road" [甘晓松：奔跑在创新路上的"阿甘"], Shaanxi Defense Industry Information Network, May 4, 2009, at http://www.jungong.net/_info/content/con-ren_12982.htm.

41 "CASC Fourth Academy Achieves Four Breakthroughs Within Two Years in New Motor R&D" [航天科技四院某新型发动机研制两年攻坚实现四大新突破], China Space News, December 27, 2010, at http://www.spacechina.com/xwzx_jcdt_Details.shtml?recno=72512. Program Manager was Fourth Academy Deputy Director Wang Jinglin [王景林] and Chief Designer was Gao Bo [高波], Director of the CASC Fourth Academy's Design Department.

42 For a good summary of China's evolving defense industrial policy, see Tai Ming Cheung, "The Remaking of the Chinese Defense Industry and the Rise of the Dual-Use Economy," Testimony Before the US-China Economic and Security Review Commission Hearing on China's Proliferation and the Impact of Trade Policy on Defense Industries in the United States and China, July 13 2007. Also see Tai Ming Cheung, "The Chinese Defense Economy's Long March from Imitation to Innovation," Study of Innovation and Technology in China, Policy Brief No. 3, September 2010, at http://igcc.ucsd.edu/research/security/SITC/SITCpolicybrief03.pdf.

43 Among various sources, see Dr. Tai Ming Cheung, "The Remaking of the Chinese Defense Industry and the Rise of the Dual-Use Economy," Testimony Before the US-China Economic and Security Review Commission, Hearing on China's Proliferation and the Impact of Trade Policy on Defense Industries in the United States and China, July 13 2007. For another good overview of China's defense industrial reforms, see Evan S. Medeiros, Roger Cliff, Keith Crane, James C. Mulvenon, A New Direction for China's Defense Industry, RAND Corporation, 2005. Also see James Mulvenon and Rebecca Samm Tyroler-Cooper, China's Defense Industry on the Path of Reform, Defense Group Inc. (DGI) Center for Intelligence Research and Analysis, Report Prepared for the US-China

Economic and Security Review Commission, October 2009, at
http://www.uscc.gov/researchpapers/2009/DGIReportonPRCDefenseIndustry--FinalVersion_10Nov2009.pdf.

44 See, for example, Mark Stokes, Appendix One and Appendix Two, "China's Evolving Conventional Strategic Strike Capability: The Anti-Ship Ballistic Missile Challenge to U.S. Maritime Operations in the Western Pacific and Beyond," Project 2049 Occasional Paper, September 2009, at
http://project2049.net/documents/chinese_anti_ship_ballistic_missile_asbm.pdf.

45 See "Company Summary" [公司简介] under "CASC" [中国航天科技集团公司] official web site, "CASC" [中国航天科技集团公司], 2011, at http://www.spacechina.com/jtgk.shtml.

46 One of the senior designers of the DF-31 was Liu Baoyong, who worked in the First Academy's First Design Department. Among the programs currently under development are said to the LM-5 and possibly a new mobile solid fuelled ICBM. For a good overview of CASC First Academy institutes and factories, see "New Starting Point, New Long March" [新起点，新长征], China Aerospace Science and Technology Corporation, undated.

47 The 10th Research Institute's director, who served as a chief designer of a major solid fueled ballistic missile system, also heads the PLA/GAD General Missile Technology Expert Working Group and serves as deputy director of the PLA/GAD Precision Guidance Expert Working Group.

48 Established in 1968, the 501st Research Institute is also known as the China Spacecraft Integrated Design Department [中国空间技术研究院总体部].

49 CAST's Dongfanghong Satellite Company [航天东方红卫星公司] appears to be a significant commercial entity. It was established in August 2001 as a wholly-owned satellite research and production subsidiary of China Spacesat. The enterprise is publicly traded company that offers satellite-related solutions to military and civil users. Its activities include manufacturing of satellite ground equipment, and satellite services, such as satellite integrated applications, satellite navigation, satellite remote sensing and image transmission, satellite communication, television broadcasting, etc. It has eight subsidiaries, including ones in Xiamen, Yungang, and Xian. Dongfanghong lays claim to the CAST968 platform as a common bus for small and microsatellites.

50 Established in 2000, Shenzhen Academy of Aerospace Technology is a joint venture between CASC, the Shenzhen City government, and Harbin Institute of Technology. It specializes in radio frequency identification (RFID), digital trunking communication systems, GPS vehicle location, radio frequency monitoring systems, as well as systems integration services.It has a relationship with a number of organizations, including the Bauman Institute in Russia, Samara State Aerospace University (SSAU), Russian Academy of Sciences (Far East Branch), Far East Technical University, Novosibirsk State Technical University, National Technical University of Ukraine, and Saint Petersburg Electrotechnical University.

51 See "Launch Services Management," CGWIC Website, at http://cn.cgwic.com/LaunchServices/index.html on 10 March 2011.

52 Xin Dingding, "China Seeks Bigger Share Of Global Satellite Market," *China Daily*, October 21, 2010 at http://www.chinadaily.com.cn/china/2010-10/21/content_11437002.htm.

53 For background on CASIC, see http://www.casic.com.cn/n16/index.html. The CEO/President of CASIC (航天科工集团) is Xu Dazhe. Born in 1956 and with roots in the CASC First Academy's 15th Research Institute and 211 Factory, Xu moved up the chain within the First Academy and CASC. He was appointed as head of the First Academy in 2000. In 2007, senior industry leadership promoted him to CASIC to assume the senior position. His senior deputy is Gao Hongwei, also born in 1956 and with roots in the 066 Base and Third Academy (cruise

missiles). Other deputies include Cheng Wen (承文), Fang Xiangming (方向明), Li Yue [李跃], and Cao Jianguo (曹建国).

54 Formed in 1978 in Nanjing, the 8511 Institute is the aerospace industry's main electronic and infrared countermeasures entity. It manages an integrated test and manufacturing facility in Nanjing's Jiangning Science Park.

55 Zhang Yiqun, assigned to the CASIC Second Academy Second Design Department, is a possible sub-system designer for the ASAT/missile defense KKV. Cited as a deputy chief designer of an unnamed system, Zhang was granted a national "model worker" award in April 2010. For one account, see "Preliminary Analysis on China's Ground-Based Mid-Course Missile Defense Intercept Technology" [中国 "陆基中段反导拦截技术试验" 初步分析], Chinese Military Network, January 13, 2010, at http://military.china.com/zh_cn/critical3/27/20100113/15774945.html.

56 The CASIC Fourth Academy director is Pan Xudong [潘旭东], who replaced the 47-year old Shen Weiwei [沈维伟] sometime in 2008. Shen had previously served as the Third Academy's Deputy Director. Yang Xiling (杨西玲) and Yang Shaohua [杨少华] are deputy directors. Unlike other academies within China's space and missile industry, few details on its executives are available.
57 The Fourth Design Department was formerly subordinate to the Second Academy, one of the few academies that has managed more than one subordinate design department.

58 "Third Line" refers to the Mao-era to create a military-industrial complex deep in the Chinese hinterlands that would survive any attacks, including nuclear ones, and sustain long-term Chinese resistance. Various armaments industries were dispersed throughout western China, often in isolated locations. For further details, see Barry Naughton, "The Third Front: Defence Industrialization in the Chinese Interior," *The China Quarterly*, 115 (Autumn, 1988), pp 351-386.

59 [熊玮 探寻人生的无限可能], *China Space News*, July 13, 2007, at http://www.china-spacenews.com/n435777/n435778/n435788/34605.html, accessed on May 29, 2010.

60 See "Making Friends with Researcher Wu Chunfeng from CASIC Ninth Academy" [航天科工集团第9研究院研究员武春风校友], Alumni Profile, Harbin Institute of Technology, at http://today.hit.edu.cn/articles/2010/06-04/0614513311.htm. Wu is an advisor to the Second Artillery on terminal seeker technology.

61 061 Base's 302 Research Institute functions as one of five software development centers under CASIC. Its core competency may be surface-to-air missile components, and thus a key supplier for CASIC Second Academy. Suzhou is located within a regional cluster of microelectronics R&D and production entities. As a supplier of components, it may face competition from other entities inside CASIC itself. For example, one manufacturing entity directly under the cognizance of CASIC headquarters, the 694 Factory (Xinyang Aerospace Fastener Co), also specializes in aerospace fasteners, with particular focus on titanium alloy technology.

62 The 068 Base opened its Near Space Flight Vehicle Development Center in 2005, and an Advanced Materials and Equipment Development Center in June 2009.

63 See "2006 China's Aerospace White Paper" [2006年中国的航天白皮书全文], China National Space Administration [国家航天局], October 12, 2006, at http://www.cnsa.gov.cn/n615708/n620168/n750545/79483.html.

64 See General Work Regulations on Weapons Systems R&D Designer System and Program Management System [武器装备研制设计师系统和行政指挥系统工作条例]. The regulations have been in place since 1984, and unlikely to have changed since then. Also see "Development and Path to Understanding Aerospace Systems "Dual Command"

Cadre" [航天型号 "两总" 团队的职业发展困惑与破解之道], CASC website, April 18, 2011, at http://www.spacechina.com/xwzx_zyxw_Details.shtml?recno=74900.

65 For example, Major General Yang Liwei (born 1965), China's first astronaut and Deputy Director of the GAD Manned Space Program Office, is the second youngest among the more than 350 full and alternate Central Committee members, and the youngest military member (youngest among full/alternate members is China Communist Youth League First Secretary Lu Hao, who was born in 1967). Born in 1961, Zhang Qingwei, Deputy Program Manager of the Shenzhou-5 and Shenzhou-6 missions, former SASTIND Director, and currently Party Chief of Hebei Province, is the fourth youngest Central Committee member and a potential Sixth Generation leader. Former CNSA Deputy Director Jin Zhuanglong (born 1964) is one of the youngest alternate members of the Central Committee. Alternate Central Committee member Liu Shiquan from 066 Base (born 1963) is yet another rising star.

66 For an excellent historical overview of China's manned space program, see Kulacki and Lewis, pp. 19-29. Among various assessments, see Joan Johnson-Freese, "Space Weiqi: The Launch of Shenzhou V," *Naval War College Review*, Spring 2004, Vol. LVII, No. 2; Fiona Cunningham, "The Stellar Status Symbol: True Motives for China's Manned Space Program," *China Security*, 2009, Issue 15, at http://www.chinasecurity.us/pdfs/FionaCunningham.pdf. For further details, see the Manned Space Program Office website at http://www.cmse.gov.cn/AboutUs/list.php?catid=9.

67 As of April 2011, former GAD Deputy Chief of Staff Major General Wang Wenbao [王文宝] directs the 921 Engineering office, and thus China's manned space program. See http://scitech.people.com.cn/GB/14383518.html. Appointed in 2008 as the office's third director since its formation in 1999, he succeeded MGen Tang Xianming [唐贤明] and Xie Mingbao [谢名苞]. Promoted his current rank in 2003, Wang Wenbao also has command GAD's 26 Base, responsible for China's satellite, tracking, and control system.

68 "China's Space Activities in 2006," China National Space Administration, 12 Dec 2006, 22 June 2011 < http://www.cnsa.gov.cn/n615709/n620682/n639462/79381.htmll>.

69 The sub-sensor designer was Jiang Dao'an [姜道安], who served as Deputy Director of the 29th Research Institute. Jiang was reportedly the chief designer of the sensor sub-system on SJ-6 pairs. Jiang has been associated with the GAD ECM Key Test Lab, which is hosted by the 29th Research Institute. He also was involved in sub-system development for the Shenzhou-2. See "Introduction of Candidates for the Sichuan Outstanding Innovation Award" [凝聚创新人才 推进 "两个加快" 第五届 "四川杰出创新人才奖" 20名候选人简介], *Sichuan Online*, January 14, 2010, at http://news.163.com/10/0114/06/5SVI1B02000120GR.html. He also is a senior defense industry advisor [军工部副主任姜道安].

70 Stephanie Lieggi and Leigh Aldrich. "China's Manned Space Program: Trajectory and Motivations," James Martin Center for Nonproliferation Studies, October 6, 2003, at http://cns.miis.edu/stories/031006.htm.

71 Wang Zhonggui, Dong Nengli, and Zhai Zhigang, "China Manned Space Flight Program," October 10, 2009, at www.thespacereview.com/archive/1565a.pdf. Qi Faren served as Chief Designer for Shenzhou-1 through Shenzhou-5. Born in June 1964, Zhang Bainan [张柏楠], from the Fifth Academy's 501 Design Department, served as Deputy Chief Designer of the Shenzhou 6 space module and Chief Designer of the Shenzhou 7 space module. He also is said to be Chief Designer for the Shenzhou 8 and Tiangong-1.

72 Morris Jones. "Tiangong Space Station Plans Progressing," *Space Daily*, 7 Dec 2010, at http://www.spacedaily.com/reports/Tiangong_Space_Station_Plans_Progessing_999.html.

73 Leading advocates included Ouyang Ziyuan and Chu Guibo. For an excellent over of the lunar program policy, see Patrick Besha, "Policy Making in China's Space Program: A History and Analysis of the Chang'e Lunar Orbiter Project," *Space Policy* 26 (2010), at http://www.gwu.edu/~spi/assets/docs/Besha_article_2010.pdf. Also see "China to Launch 2nd Lunar Probe Before End of 2011," *Xinhua*, November 12, 2008, at http://www.chinadaily.com.cn/china/2008-11/12/content_7199005.htm. For reference to potential of Helium-3, see John Lasker, "Race to the Moon for Nuclear Fuel," *Wired*, December 15, 2006, at http://www.wired.com/science/space/news/2006/12/72276.

74 See, for example, CAS Lunar Exploration Engineer Department Job Listing [中国科学院探月工程总体部招聘启事], CAS website, February 14, 2011, at http://www.cas.cn/rc/rczp/201102/t20110214_3071119.shtml. Also see "Integrated Lunar Exploration Engineering Organization Management" [绕月探测工程组织管理], MIIT website, at http://www.miit.gov.cn/n11293472/n11293877/n12079125/n12079351/12082808.html. Other organizations represented in the Leading Group include the National Development and Reform Commission (NDRC), Ministry of Science and Technology (MOST), General Armaments Department (GAD), China Academy of Sciences (CAS), and China Aerospace Science and Technology Corporation (CASC). Directing the SASTIND Engineering Office (and overall program manager) is Hu Hao [胡浩]. Subordinate entities include an integrated management department, planning and finance department, engineering management department, and technology development department. Among the four deputy program managers is GAD Deputy Director Niu Hongguang [牛红光]. Others include Yin Hejun [阴和俊] from CAS, Wang Zhigang [王志刚] from Ministry of Science and Technology, and Ma Xingrui [马兴瑞] and Yuan Jiajun [袁家军] from CASC. CASC's Wu Weiren [吴伟仁] serves as the lunar exploration program's Chief Designer. Wu Weiren has roots in the CASC 210 Factory, responsible for manufacturing of navigation, control, and attitude control systems and components, including satellite navigation, tracking and telemetry.

75 "China's Space Program: Civilian, Commercial, and Military Aspects," <http://www.highfrontier.org/Archive/hf/Finkelstein%20China's%20Space%20Program.pdf>.

76 These included a high-energy sun particle detector, laser altimeter, microprobe instruments, three-dimensional charge-coupled device (CCD) cameras, gamma and x-ray spectrometer, and microwave radiometer. Among various sources, see Ouyang Ziyuan, "The Scientific Objectives of Chinese Lunar Exploration Project, presentation before the 9th International Symposium on Physical Measurements and Signature in Remote Sensing (ISPMSRS), Beijing, China, October 17-19, 2005, at http://www.geog.umd.edu/ispmsrs2005/OuyangZiyuanAbs.htm. Ouyang is with the China Academy of Sciences' National Astronomical Observatory.

77 Huang Jiangchuan [黄江川] is said to be the Chang'e-2's Chief Designer. Born in August 1961, Huang served as a systems engineering within the Fifth Academy (CAST) 502nd Research Institute, and had previously served as Deputy Chief Designer of the Chang-e-1 system.

78 Ibid.

79 China Expects to Launch Lunar Probe Chang'e 5 in 2017," *NASA Lunar Science Institute*, 2 March 2011, at http://lunarscience.arc.nasa.gov/articles/china-expects-to-launch-lunar-probe-change-5-in-2017>.

80 Bruce Sterling, "Chinese Manned Moon Landing, 2025," 19 September 2010, at http://www.wired.com/beyond_the_beyond/2010/09/chinese-manned-moon-landing-2025/>.

81 "China to Accept Private Funding for Lunar Missions," *Space Daily*, 8 Nov 2007, at http://www.spacedaily.com/reports/China_to_accept_private_funding_for_lunar_missions_999.html.

[82] David Leonard, "China's First Space Station: A New Foothold in Earth Orbit," Space.com, 6 May 2011, 27 May 2011 <http://www.space.com/11592-china-space-station-tiangong-details.html>.

[83] Clara Moscowicz, "China Shifts Space Station Project into Overdrive," *Space.com*, 15 April 2010 at http://www.space.com/8224-china-shifts-space-station-project-overdrive.html.

[84] "Launch of China's Manned Spacecraft Shenzhou-9 Scheduled," Xinhua, February 17, 2012, at http://english.cntv.cn/20120217/115356.shtml.

[85] Clay Dillow, "China Announces Plan to Build a Manned Space Station of its own Within Ten Years," *Popular Science*, 26 April 2011, 27 June 2011 <http://www.popsci.com/technology/article/2011-04/china-plans-build-manned-space-station-its-own-within-ten-years>.

[86] Tania Branigan, "China Unveils Rival to International Space Station," *The Guardian*, 26 Apr 2010 at http://www.guardian.co.uk/world/2011/apr/26/china-space-station-tiangong.

[87] Clara Moscowicz, "China's Lofty Goals: Space Station, Moon, and Mars Exploration," *Space.com*, 6 Dec 2010, 27 June 2011 <http://www.space.com/166-china-lofty-goals-space-station-moon-mars-exploration.html>.

[88] David Cyranoski, "China unveils its space station," Naturenews, May 4, 2011, at http://www.nature.com/news/2011/110504/full/473014a.html.

[89] For a summary of militarily-relevant aspects of space-based sensors, see Andrew S. Erickson, "Satellites Support Growing PLA Maritime Monitoring and Targeting Capabilities," Jamestown China Brief, Vol 11, Issue 3, February 10,2011, at http://www.jamestown.org/single/?no_cache=1&tx_ttnews%5Btt_news%5D=37490&tx_ttnews%5BbackPid%5D=7&cHash=20e0b222a8c961508f37fa5b72ad1925.

[90] For one widely cited article published 10 years ago, see Ma Genhai, "Considerations Regarding China's Military Use Satellite System Entering the Next Century," *Journal of the Institute of Command and Control Technology* (*Zhihui jishu xueyuan xuebao*), 1999, Vol. 10, No. 6. Also see Zhu Bin and Chen Xuan, "A Space-Based Electronic Information System for Long-range Precision Strike," *Aerospace China*, 2007, Issue 3.

[91] Qiu and Long assert that a program to deploy a space-based reconnaissance architecture, programmed under the 863 program for 2015-2020, was advanced in 2004. The total scope of the space architecture is unknown at the current time. However, in their 2006/7 *Modern Ships* article, Qiu and Long assess that during a crisis, 24 satellites could be available, including six EO satellites, 10 radar reconnaissance satellites, two maritime satellites, and six electronic reconnaissance satellites with a visit rate of 40 minutes. For emergencies, microsatellites, with a life of 1-2 weeks, can augment large ones and be launched from mobile platforms within 12 hours of an order.

[92] "China Blasts Off First Data Relay Satellite," *Xinhua News Agency*, April 26, 2008. For an example of the data relay satellite being used for missile guidance, see Chen Lihu, Wang Shilian, Zhang Eryang, "Modeling and Simulation Of Missile Satellite-Missile Link Channel In Flying-Control Data-Link" (基于卫星中继的导弹飞控数据链链路分析), *Systems Engineering And Electronics*, 29(6), 2007. The chief designer of the satellite was Ye Peijian [叶培建]. Also see Wu Ting-yong, Wu Shi-qi, Ling Xiang, "A MEO Tracking and Data Relay Satellite System Constellation Scheme for China," *Journal of Electronic Science and Technology of China*, December 2005.

[93] See, for example, Huang Hanwen, "Conceptual Study on Stealth Satellites [卫星隐身概念研究], *Aerospace Electronic Countermeasures* [航天电子对抗], June 2010, pp. 22-34. Huang is from the Shanghai Academy of Space Technology's 509 Research Institute.

94 See Wu Weiqi and Zhang Yulin, "The Preliminary Study of General Effectiveness Model of the Ocean Target Detection Satellite System" [海洋目标探测卫星的通用效能模型初探], *Journal of Astronautics* [宇航学报], Vol. 27, No. 4, 2006; Wu Weiqi and Zhang Yulin, "Agent-based Simulation Method for Performance Evaluation of Satellite System" [基于Agent的卫星体系效能评估仿真方法], *Computer Simulation* [计算机仿真], Vol. 24, No. 7, 2007; Wu Weiqi and Zhang Yulin, "Analysis on the Probability of Target Detection with Photo-reconnaissance Satellite" [光学侦察卫星的目标探测概率分析], *Journal of National University of Defense Technology* [国防科技大学学报], Vol. 28, No. 4, 2006; and Wu Weiqi and Zhang Yulin, "SAR Satellite Baseline Mean Direction Optimization and Design" [星载In SAR空间基线指向优化与设计], *Chinese Journal of Space Science* [空间科学学报], Volume 26, No. 3, 2006. Major General Zhang Yulin is former Commander, Jiuquan Satellite Launch Center and a senior GAD authority on space and space launch systems.

95 "National Remote Sensing Center" [国家遥感中心], Ministry of Science and Technology website, undated, at http://www.most.gov.cn/zzjg/zzjgzs/zzjgsyygzx/index.htm.

96 "Yaogan series (China), Spacecraft – Defense," *Jane's Space Systems and Industry*, August 18, 2010, at http://www.janes.com/articles/Janes-Space-Systems-and-Industry/Yaogan-series-China.html.

97 "Successful Launch of the Yaogan-2" [我国成功发射 "遥感卫星二号"], Xinhua, May 25, 2007, at http://news.xinhuanet.com/politics/2007-05/25/content_6152111.htm. A key designer of the Yaogan-2's high resolution camera system was Yang Bingxin [杨秉新]. See [杨秉新：遥感星空的一颗启明星], China Space News, undated, at http://www.spacechina.com/qywh_htrw_Details.shtml?recno=60959. Yang is from the 508th Research Institute.

98 Follow-on variants of the Yaogan-2 may include Yaogan-4, Yaogan-7, and Yaogan-11. A follow-on variant of the Yaogan-5 may include the Yaogan-12.

99 Chen Xiaoli and Yang Bingxin, [实现甚高分辨率空间遥感器的可展开光学系统], paper presented before the 17th Conference of the China Space Science Association, 2004. See previous reference for background on Yang Bingxin.

100 Chen Deyuan and Tu Guofang, "SAR Image Enhancement Using Multi-scale Products for Targets Detection, Remote Sensing Journal [*Yaogan xuebao]),* March 2007, pp. 185-192. Authors are from the Institute of Electronics, Chinese Academy of Sciences.

101 Chen Deyuan and Tu Guofang, "SAR Image Enhancement Using Multi-scale Products for Targets Detection, Remote Sensing Journal [*Yaogan xuebao]),* March 2007, pp. 185-192. Authors are from the Institute of Electronics, Chinese Academy of Sciences.

102 While not 100% certain, the lead systems integrator for SAR satellites appears to be the Shanghai Academy of Space Technology. The SAR package likely is the responsibility of the China Academy of Sciences Institute of Electronics. Shanghai also designed, developed, and manufactured the LM-4 series of launch vehicles, which generally are used for sun synchronous orbit satellites and launched from the Taiyuan Space Launch Center. The LM-4B program manager was Li Xiangrong [李相荣]. For an early discussion on the dual nature aspects of SAR satellites, see Huang Weiken, Zhou Changbao, "Outlook and Requirements for China's Maritime SAR Satellites," *China Aerospace* [*Zhongguo hangtian*], 1997(12).

103 Guo Huadong, "Spaceborne and Airborne SAR for Target Detection and Flood Monitoring," *Photogrammetric Engineering and Remote Sensing*, May 2000 (in English). The lead organization for basic research and developmental work is said to be the China Academy of Sciences Institute of Electronics. Also see Zhu Minhui and Wu Yirong, "Extend Progresses in Synthetic Aperture Radar Technology," paper presented at the Asian

Conference on Remote Sensing 1999 (in English). The on-board SAR processor was said to be a joint project between the Beijing Remote Sensing Institute and the Radar Systemtechnik (RST) in Switzerland.

[104] Eventually, the constellation would grow to six and five respectively. "China to Set Up World's First Satellite Constellation for Disaster Monitoring," *People's Daily*, June 25, 2004. Also see Xingling Wang; Gang Wang; Yan Guan; Quan Chen; Lianru Gao, "Small Satellite Constellation for Disaster Monitoring in China," Geoscience and Remote Sensing Symposium, 2005. IGARSS Proceedings, 2005, IEEE International, Vol 1, Issue , 25-29 July 2005, p. 3 (in English). The SAR satellites would operate in the S-Band portion of the frequency spectrum. Also see "Remote Sensing Satellites," CGWIC website (undated), at http://www.cgwic.com/In-OrbitDelivery/RemoteSensingSatellite/damage.html.

[105] With cooperation in the area of SAR satellites having been initiated as far back as 1989, the antenna was a topic of discussion during the visit of China Academy of Sciences President to Moscow in 2004. Another topic of the meeting was results of Russian Venus observation mission. Venus observation was used by the Russians in the 1970s and 1980s as a platform for testing RORSAT capabilities. *See* "Chinese Academy of Sciences Delegation's Trip to Russia is a Success," *China Academy of Sciences New Release,* July 16, 2004. The specific type of is described as a "net shaped" antenna [合成孔径雷达系统网状抛物面天线].

[106] The dimensions of the SAR satellite is 1.2m x 1.1m x 3.0 meters. The antenna is 6m x 2.8m. Its ground resolution is 20 meters, although this presumably depends on a range of factors. Its maximum resolution is said to be 5 meters.

[107] The Yaogan-1 has also been referred to as the Jianbing-5 [尖兵5号].   The Chief Designer is believed to be Eighth Academy's Wei Zhongquan. See "Wei Zhongquan – Lifetime Infatuation with Satellites" [魏钟铨一生痴情伴卫星], *China Space News*, November 14, 2008, at http://www.china-spacenews.com/n435777/n435778/n435788/50619.html. Also see http://www.cnsa.gov.cn/n1081/n7604/102769.html. The satellite has been described as an "all weather, all day, high resolution earth observation remote sensing satellite" [全天候、全天时、高分辨率对地观测遥感卫星]. Li Zhengjun [李正军] is said to have been a key designer for the antenna system.

[108] Space industry publications highlight chief designers and program managers affiliated with SAR-related research. One leading figure in early Eighth Academy SAR research was Yuan Xiaokang [袁孝康]. Yaogan-1 Chief Designer is said to be the CASC Eighth Academy 509 Research Institute's Chen Junli [陈筠力]. Born in 1972, Chen was also the Chief Designer for the Yaogan-6. For examples of Chen Junli's SAR-related research, see Chen Junli, Xu Min, and Zhu Jie, "Yaw Steering and Accuracy Requirement of Distribution SAR Satellites" [分布式SAR卫星偏航控制及精度要求], *Spacecraft Engineering*, 2008 17(1), at http://d.wanfangdata.com.cn/periodical_htqgc200801008.aspx; and Jiang Yan, Chen Junli, Wang Yun, and Wang Wenfeng, "Satellite-Borne SAR GMTI Technology [星载SAR的GMTI技术], *Aerospace Shanghai*, 2009 26(6), at http://d.wanfangdata.com.cn/Periodical_shht200906013.aspx. A Deputy Chief Designer was Fan Jixia [范季夏]. Zi Mo (ed.), "A Conversation with the Shanghai Aerospace Bureau's Zhu Hongchang, Chief Director of the Yaogan-3" [对话上海航天局遥感卫星三号总指挥朱鸿昌], Changsanjiao City Net, September 9, 2009, at http://www.cncsj.net/a/2009/9/9/content_68714.html. Another key figure was Zhu Hongchang, who has been involved in the Fengyun-2 meteorological satellite in GEO, the CBERS ZY-1 remote sensing satellite program, and the DFH-3. Also see You Benfeng, "Wei Zhongquan: A Lifetime Infatuated with Satellites"[魏钟铨一生痴情伴卫星], November 17, 2009; and Zi Mo (ed.), "A Conversation with the Shanghai Aerospace Bureau's Zhu Hongchang, Chief Director of the Yaogan-3" [对话上海航天局遥感卫星三号总指挥朱鸿昌], September 9, 2009. For reference to the Yaogan-6(2), see [第15届 "中国青年五四奖章" 初评入围人选公示], Xinhua, April 15, 2011, at http://news.xinhuanet.com/politics/2011-04/15/c_121308039_9.htm. Chen Junli is Chief Designer.

[109] Zhou Weimin [周伟敏] from the CASC Eighth Academy served as Program Manager and Hou Jianwen [侯建文] served as Chief Designer. See [遥感卫星八号吃透技术 如履薄冰把握关键], *China Space News*, December 16, 2009, at http://en.spacechina.com/xwzx_jcdt_Details.shtml?recno=64027. Hou was responsible for the attitude control system on the SJ-6 and served as Chief Designer on the SJ-7, which was launched from Jiuquan on an LM-2D in 2005.

[110] See "CASC Eighth Academy Successfully Launches Yaogan-10 Satellite" [航天八院为遥感卫星十号发射成功奋战发射场], MOST website, November 1, 2010, at http://kjj.boluo.gov.cn/show.asp?id=481.

[111] For early assessments on the utility of space-based electronic reconnaissance systems, see Yuan Xiaokang, "Satellite Electronic Reconnaissance, Antijamming," *Shanghai Hangtian*, October 9, 1996, pp. 32-37, in *FBIS-CST*-97-011; and Yuan Xiaokang, "Some Problems of Space Electronic Reconnaissance," *Hangtian Dianzi Duikang*, March 1996, pp. 1-5, in *CAMA*, Vol. 3, No. 4. Yuan is a key engineer involved space-based antenna systems design, including both ELINT and SAR, from the SAST 509th Research Institute (Shanghai Institute of Satellite Engineering).

[112] See Pan Changpeng, Gu Wenjin and Chen Jie, "An Analysis on the Capabilities of Military Satellites to Support an ASBM in Offense and Defense Operations" [军事卫星对反舰导弹攻防作战的支援能力分析], 2006, No. 5. See also Gao Fei, Hu Xujie, Gao Lingyuan, and Liu Xiangmin, "An Analysis on the Influence of Military Satellite Information Systems on Missile Operations" [军事卫星信息系统对导弹作战的影响分析], Vol. 29, No. 4, 2008; Hu Xujie, Liu Zhiyuan, Wang Mo, Sun Yu, and Qiao Tian, An Analysis on the Effectiveness of Space-based Information to Support Missile Offense and Defense Operations" [天基信息支援对导弹攻防作战的效用分析], Vol. 18, No. 1, 2009; and Huang Xuan, Zeng Jiayou, Zhao Xu Ming, and Niu Liyong, "Graph Modeling Influence of Space-based Information Supporting Aerospace Force Anti-ship Missile Assault" [天基信息支援下航空兵对海导弹攻击的影响图模型], Vol. 2, 2007.

[113] *Defense Science Board Task Force on the Future Of The Aircraft Carrier*, OSD/AT&L, October 2002, pp. 52-53

[114] The GSD ECM and Radar Department (GSD Fourth Department) has the ELINT portfolio within the PLA's SIGINT apparatus. This department is responsible for electronic countermeasures, requiring them to collect and maintain data bases on electronic signals. ELINT receivers are the responsibility of the Southwest Institute of Electronic Equipment (SWIEE). The GSD 54th Research Institute supports the ECM Department in development of digital ELINT signal processors to analyze parameters of radar pulses. See Ping Kefu, "Capabilities of The GSD Third Department in Technical Intelligence," *East Asian Diplomacy and Defense Review*, 96 (5), p. 6. Information on China's SIGINT apparatus drawn from Desmond Ball, "Signals Intelligence in China," *Jane's Intelligence Review*, August 1, 1995, pp. 365-375; and Robert Karniol, "China Sets Up Border SIGINT Bases In Laos," *Jane's Defense Weekly*, November 19, 1994, p. 5.

[115] Also see Yuan Xiaokang, "Satellite Electronic Reconnaissance, Antijamming," *Shanghai Hangtian*, October 9, 1996, pp. 32-37, in *FBIS-CST*-97-011; and Yuan Xiaokang, "Some Problems of Space Electronic Reconnaissance," *Hangtian Dianzi Duikang*, March 1996, pp. 1-5, in *CAMA*, Vol. 3, No. 4. Yuan is a key engineer involved space-based antenna systems design, including both ELINT and SAR, from the SAST 509th Research Institute (Shanghai Institute of Satellite Engineering).

[116] Li Wenhua, "Research on Configuring Three-Satellites and Time Difference of Arrival for Precise Geo-Location" [三星构型设计与时差定位精度研究], *Journal of Astronautics* [宇航学报], March 2010, pp. 701-705. The author is affiliated with the Jiangnan Electronic Communication Institute in Jiaxing; and Li Jianjun, "Research on Four-Satellite TDOA Location Algorithm" [四星时差定位算法研究], *Electronic Warfare Technology* [电子对抗技术], July 2004, p. 3. The author is affiliated with the Southwest China Research Institute of Electronic Equipment (29th

Research Institute) in Chengdu; Gao Qian, Guo Fucheng, Wu Jing, Jiang Wenli, "A Correcting Algorithm of Single Source Reference Source for Three-Satellite TDOA Location System" [一种三星时差定位系统的校正算法研究], *Aerospace Electronic Warfare* [航天电子对抗], Vol. 23, No.5, 2007. The authors are affiliated with the National University of Defense Technology. Wu Shilong, Zhao Yongsheng, and Luo Jingqing, "Performance Analysis of Two-Satellite Joint FDOA and TDOA Location System" [双星时差频差联合定位系统性能分析], *Aerospace Shanghai* [上海航空], No. 2, 2007, p. 47. Wu and Zhao are affiliated with GSD Fourth Department 61541 Unit in Beijing, and Luo is affiliated with the PLA Electronic Engineering Institute in Hefei. The 61541 Unit is said to be located in "Space City" [航天城] north of Zhongguancun section of Beijing, appears to serve as an information fusion and R&D center, focusing on phased lock loop (PLL) receiving technology among other issues.

[117] Huang Hanwen, "Maritime Target Surveillance Satellite System Analysis and Development Assumptions" [卫星海洋目标监视系统分析与发展设想], *Journal of the Academy of Equipment Command & Technology* [装备指挥技术学院学报], October 2004, pp. 44-48, at http://d.wanfangdata.com.cn/periodical_zhjsxy200405011.aspx. The author is affiliated with the Shanghai Institute of Satellite Engineering, or SAST 509th Research Institute. Also see Gao Fei, Hu Xujie, Gao Lingyuan, and Liu Xiangmin, "An Analysis on the Influence of Military Satellite Information Systems on Missile Operations" [军事卫星信息系统对导弹作战的影响分析], *National Defense Science and Technology* [国防科技], Vol. 29, No. 4, 2008; Hu Xujie, Liu Zhiyuan, Wang Mo, Sun Yu, and Qiao Tian, An Analysis on the Effectiveness of Space-based Information to Support Missile Offense and Defense Operations" [天基信息支援对导弹攻防作战的效用分析], *Spacecraft Engineering* [航空器工程], Vol. 18, No. 1, 2009; and Huang Xuan, Zeng Jiayou, Zhao Xu Ming, and Niu Liyong, "Graph Modeling Influence of Space-based Information Supporting Aerospace Force Anti-ship Missile Assault" [天基信息支援下航空兵对海导弹攻击的影响图模型], *Tactical Missile Technology* [战术导弹技术], Vol. 2, 2007.

[118] Wang Huilin, Huang Wei, Ma Manhao, and Zhu Xiaomin, "Design and Implementation of Area-Covering Electronic Reconnaissance Satellite Planning System" [面向区域的电子侦察卫星规划系统设计与实现], *Computer Engineering and Applications* [计算机工程与应用], Vol. 46, No. 26, 2010, pp. 209. The authors are affiliated with the National University of Defense Technology's National Key C4ISR Technology Laboratory in Changsha. Their research was conducted as part of the 973 Program.

[119] Dong Qiaozhong and Zhu Weiqiang, "Research on ELINT Satellite Techniques in GSO" [静止轨道电子侦察卫星技术研究], *Electronic Warfare* [电子对抗], July 30, 2009, p. 13. The authors are affiliated with the CASIC 8511 Research Institute in Nanjing; Lu An'nan, "Thoughts on Developmental Problems of ELINT Satellite Passive Geo-location Techniques" [对电子侦察卫星无源定位技术发展问题的思考], *Communications Countermeasures* [通信对抗], March 2008, pp. 19-20. The author is affiliated with the 36th Research Institute of CETC in Jiaxing, Zhejiang; Li Hengnian, Gao Yijun, Xu Peijun, Li Jisheng, and Huang Yongxuan, "The Strategies and Algorithm Study For Multi-GEO Satellite Collocation" [地球静止轨道共位控制策略研究], *Journal of Astronautics* [宇航学报], Vol. 30, No. 3, 2009. Also see Dong Qiaozhong and Zhu Weiqiang, "Study on Electronic Reconnaissance Satellites in Geostationary Orbit" [静止轨道电子侦察卫星技术研究], *Electronic Countermeasures*, June 2009, at http://www.cqvip.com/qk/91679x/200906/32557007.html. The authors are from the CASIC 8511 Research Institute in Nanjing.

[120] China SpaceSat Company appears to serve as a CAST commercial front. See "Shijian-6 Tandem Twin Launch Successful" [实践六号双星发射成功], *China Spacesat Company* [中国东方红卫星股份有限公司], October 8, 2010, at http://www.spacesat.com.cn/newdfh/xwzx/ArticleShow.asp?ArticleID=260. Also see "Foreign Military Observers' Interpretations: China's ELINT Satellite Plans" [外国军事观察家另类解读-中国电子情报卫星计划], November 15, 2004.

121 Responsible for the A satellite, Shen Cong [沈琼] had previously worked on programs previously believed to be related to electronic reconnaissance in the 1970s. CASC Fifth Academy's Wu Kailin [吴开林] was Chief Designer of the SJ-6B satellite [实践六号B], which operated in conjunction with the SJ-6A. 121

122 Chen Xingquan, "Shen Cong: Trial and Hardships on the Road to Space" [沈琼：风云程巡天路], *China Aerospace Science and Technology Corporation (CASIC)*, at http://www.spacechina.com/qywh_htrw_Details.shtml?recno=36670.

123 Born in 1970 and assigned to the Shanghai Academy of Space Technology (SAST, or Eighth Academy), Chen Zhansheng [陈占胜] was Chief Designer for the SJ-12 satellite. He also had served as Deputy Chief Designer of the SJ-6 and served as Executive Assistant to the Director, 509th Research Institute. He also spent time with Aerospatial for training in satellite engineering. See" For China's Most Beautiful Satellite: Commemorating Shanghai Aerospace' S&T Committee's Chen Zhansheng" [为了最美的'中国星：' 记上海航天局科技委常委陈占胜], Worker.cn, April 28, 2011, at http://character.workercn.cn/c/2011/04/28/110428095902614394971.html; http://www.gov.cn/jrzg/2010-06/15/content_1628088.htm. and http://210.82.31.84:9000/rp/fs/cp/98/36/20100618/4/icontent_0.htm.

124 See Brian Weeden, " Dancing in the Dark: The Orbital Rendezvous of SJ-12 and SJ-06F, *The Space Review*, August 30, 2010, at http://www.thespacereview.com/article/1689/1.

125 The formation orbits in a 1080 km x 1100 km x 63.4 degree position, strikingly reminiscent of earlier generations of the U.S. "White Cloud" NOSS satellite triplets described in detail by Chinese writings. Among various sources, see "China's Yaogan-9 may be ocean surveillance satellite," *Jane's Defense Weekly*, March 11, 2010, at http://www.janes.com/articles/Janes-Defence-Weekly-2010/China-s-Yaogan-9-may-be-ocean-surveillance-satellite.html. The initial indication that the *Yaogan*-9 may be a NOSS system came from a number of amateur astronomers who reported that the *Yaogan*-9 mission saw the launch of not one, but rather a constellation of three satellites that are now orbiting together in a highly choreographed triangular formation. For example see: "Yaogan 9A, 9B, 9C," *Gunter's Space Page*, undated, at http://space.skyrocket.de/doc_sdat/yaogan-9.htm; "Yaogan Weixing-9 CZ-4C launch March 5, 2010," *NASA Spaceflight.com*, March 5, 2010, at http://forum.nasaspaceflight.com/index.php?topic=20567.30, accessed December 9, 2010; and Robert Christy, "Space Events of 2010," *Zarya*, undated, at http://www.zarya.info/Diaries/2010.php. Yaogan Weixing 9," *Jonathan's Space Report*, No. 625, April 6, 2010, at http://planet4589.org/space/jsr/back/news.625.

126 The Program Manager and Chief Designer of the Yaogan-9 was Li Yandong [李延东]. Space industry reporting indicates that the Yaogan-9 program took four years to complete. Li Yandong also served as the director and chief designer of one of the two Shijian-6 Group-04 satellites, and was previously involved in China's Haiyang-1 maritime surveillance satellite program. See "Warm Celebrations: 'Yaogan-9' Successfully Launched" [热烈庆祝："遥感九号"成功发射], China Spacesat Company [中国东方红卫星股份有限公司], March 9, 2010, at http://www.spacesat.com.cn/newdfh/xwzx/ArticleShow.asp?ArticleID=240; Li Guanjiao et al., "Open Doors to Success: Behind the Yaogan-9 Satellite Launch Success" [叩开成功之门——遥感卫星九号发射见闻], *China Space News*, March 10, 2010, at http://www.china-spacenews.com/n435777/n435778/n435783/66907.html; See: Xing Wen, "Li Yandong: Overcoming Difficulties and Dreams of Small Satellites" [李延东 攻坚克难 逐梦小卫星], *China Aerospace Science and Technology Corporation* (CASC), October 29, 2010, at http://www.spacechina.com/zt_chxzy/dyfc_Details.shtml?recno=71056. See also: "Li Yandong" [李延东], *Xinhua*, October 10, 2007, at http://www.gs.xinhuanet.com/jdwt/2007-10/10/content_11364907.htm.

127 For reference to the GSD Fourth Department ground stations in Shandong, see Yuan Zuzheng, "Ceng Weihua's Story – The Director's 'Hard Headedness'" ["曾卫华故事集——部长的 '执着面'"], Renminwang, September 21, 2009, at http://military.people.com.cn/GB/8221/71065/169352/169355/10091206.html. Ceng Weihua was former Jinan

Military Region Communications Department Director. Other candidates include the GSD Fourth Department 96714 Unit in Beijing and Hainan; 61764 Unit in Hainan, 61276 Unit in Beijing and Hainan, or 61541 Unit in Beijing.

[128] Oceanographic monitoring is a focus area within the 863 Program, specifically the maritime area [海洋领域]. Also see http://www.cgwic.com/In-OrbitDelivery/RemoteSensingSatellite/SEA.html.

[129] Jiang Xingwei, Lin Mingsen, and Tang Junwu, "The Programs of China Ocean Observation Satellites and Applications," National Satellite Ocean Application Service briefing, February 26, 2008 (in English).

[130] See "China to Launch FY-4 Weather Satellite Around 2013," *Xinhua News Agency*, October 14, 2008, accessed November 3, 2011, at http://www.spacedaily.com/reports/China_To_Launch_FY_4_Weather_Satellite_Around_2013_999.html.

[131] "Premier Zhou En-lai: We Shall Establish Our Own Weather Satellites," [周恩来总理提出 "要搞我们自己的气象卫星"], China Meteorological Newspaper [中国气象报社], March 15, 2011, at http://www.cma.gov.cn/ztbd/20110104/20110314/2011031405/201103/t20110315_88685.html.

[132] See "Delivery of Four FY-3 Payloads and Satellite Testing" [风云三号气象卫星4项有效载荷交付总体装星测试], *Sina News*, August 8, 2006, accessed January 20, 2012, http://tech.sina.com.cn/d/2006-08-08/15291076129.shtml.

[133] "The First Satellite in Fengyun-3 Series to Be Launched in 2006" [风云三号系列的第一颗卫星将于2006年发射], *Xinhua*, March 23, 2004, at http://news.qq.com/a/20040323/000009.htm.

[134] See the official FY-3 program website at http://www.cnsa.gov.cn/n615708/n676979/n2237254/index.html.

[135] See "FY-3 Satellite Lead Designer Dong Yaohai: FY-3B to Launch In 2010" [风云三号卫星总设计师董瑶海校友：风云三号B星将于2010年发射], Harbin Institute of Technology, December 9, 2008, http://news.hit.edu.cn/articles/2008/12-09/12083258.htm, accessed January 25, 2012.

[136] See [风云三号（FY-3）气象卫星数据接收系统DPT接收12米天线分系统], http://qxfw.fjqx.gov.cn/qxkp/qxgcyq/qxwxdmjs/201112/t20111226_8801.htm. For other background on Third Department and the 39th Research Institute, see http://www.hljrm.com.cn/xw/wl/059.htm. See http://144.214.150.11/viewpage.php?tid=159&pid=267&fm=text.

[137]" See "The Successful Launch of FY-3 to Enhance Xinjiang Weather Prediction" [风云三号发射成功新疆天气预报更加准确], Xinjiang Daily, May 29, 2008, at http://www.chinaxinjiang.cn/news/xjxw/kjtw/t20080529_347501.htm.

[138] The commercial name of the 503rd Research Institute is Spacestar Technology Company. See http://www.spacestar.com.cn/contact-us.php. See "FY-3 Satellite And Ground Application Systems Second Wireless Docking Experiment" [风云三号卫星与地面应用系统进行第二次无线对接试验], Urumqi Municipal Bureau of Meteorology [乌鲁木齐市气象局], January 3, 2008, , http://www.xjqx.gov.cn/avow/DisplayContent.aspx?Number=6642; also see link http://144.214.150.11/viewpage.php?tid=159&pid=267&fm=text.

139 See "The Successful Launch of FY-3 to Enhance Xinjiang Weather Prediction" [风云三号发射成功 新疆天气预报更加准确], Xinjiang Daily, May 29, 2008, at http://www.chinaxinjiang.cn/news/xjxw/kjtw/t20080529_347501.htm. accessed January 25, 2012.

140 "Theory and Application of Collection and Fusion of Information Regarding Complex Natural Environments" [复杂自然环境时空定量信息获取与融合处理的理论与应用], Fudan University Project Overview, June 2004, at http://www.guochengzhi.com/gx/Print.asp?ArticleID=371.

141 Lu Mingyu, Yi Kui, Yang Junfa, and Deng Ruzhen, "Development of Signal Source for Real-Time Infrared Earth Sensor" [一种实时红外地球敏感器信号源的研制], *Zhongguo Kongjian Kexue Jishu*, June 1996, pp. 63-70.

142 According to a recent article published on the CAS Shanghai Institute of Technical Physics website, Chu Junhao [褚君浩], China already have developed infrared wavelengths at 1-3, 3-5 and 8-14 microns that are installed its Fengyun satellites. See "A Good Helper in Developing a Smart City – Infrared Sensors" [建设智慧城市的好帮手 – 红外线传感器], Shanghai Institute of Technical Physics of the Chinese Academy of Sciences [上海技术物理研究所], April 27, 2011, at http://www.sitp.cas.cn/kxcb/kpwz/201104/t20110427_3122606.html.

143 Under the "dual command" system, Huang Weiyi served as Program Manager and Hou Jianwen as Chief Designer. Born in 1960, Hou Jianwen is with the Shanghai Academy of Space Technology and SJ-7 Chief Designer. Hou has roots in SAST's 812 Research Institute as an attitude control specialist. He also was responsible for the SJ-6 attitude control sub-system. With a design life of three years, the SJ-7 satellite was for "space environmental monitoring and other space scientific experiments."

144 The SJ-7 orbits at an altitude of 547-570 km in a 97.6 degree inclination. Hou Jianwen [侯建文] was Chief Designer. Among various sources, see http://news.xinhuanet.com/photo/2005-07/06/content_3180927.htm.

145 http://top.jschina.com.cn/viewthread.php?tid=28949.

146 For background on the ZY-3, see "China's First High Resolution Satellite Scheduled for Launch in 2011" [我国首颗民用高分辨率卫星将于 2011 年], *China Space News*, August 4, 2010. The chief designer of the satellite system is Tang Xinming [唐新明]. Born in 1966, Tang is with the State Bureau of Survey and Mapping.

147 See "LM-4B Successfully Launches ZY-3 and VesselSat-2 Satellites," CGWIC News Release, January 2012, at http://www.cgwic.com/news/2012/0110_VesselSat-2_%E5%8D%A2%E6%A3%AE%E5%A0%A1_%E6%90%AD%E8%BD%BD.html.

148 Among various sources, see David S. Alberts, John J. Garstka, and Frederick P. Stein. *Network Centric Warfare*, (Wash DC: DoD C4ISR Cooperative Research Program, September 1999. For another outstanding overview of network centric warfare, see Clay Wilson, *Network Centric Operations: Background and Oversight Issues for Congress*, Congressional Research Service Report to Congress, March 15, 2007. In accordance with Metcalf's Law, the value" or power of a network increases in proportion to the square of the number of nodes on the network. Technology is advancing to the point to where a common operational picture could be used on a personal display assistant (PDA). At least one key organization involved in data link development is the PLA's University of Science and Technology's Command Automation Academy [解放军理工大学,指挥自动化学院], which is associated with the GSD 63rd Research Institute.

149 See Kulacki and Lewis, pp. 14-19.

150 See Roger Cliff, Chad J.R. Ohlandt, and David Yang, Ready for Take-Off: China's Advancing Aerospace Industry (Santa Monica, CA: RAND Corporation, 2011), p. 93.

151 http://www.cgwic.com/In-OrbitDelivery/CommunicationsSatellite/DFH-4Bus.html.

152 Sun Jiadong is said to have played a leading role in the Fenghuo satellite. Chief Designer of the Fenghuo is said to be Peng Shoucheng [彭守诚]. Peng has a background in the 504th Research Institute and has a background in electronic reconnaissance. Chief Designer of the Shentong-1 was Wang Jiasheng [王家胜]. Born in 1953, Wang served as deputy chief designer of the DFH-3 COMSAT and Chief Designer of the Tianlian-1 data relay satellite.

153 "China Blasts Off First Data Relay Satellite," Xinhua News Agency, April 26, 2008; and "China Successfully Launches First Data Relay Satellite, the Tianlian-1 (01)" [中国首颗数据中继卫星"天链一号01星"发射成功], Xinhua, April 26, 2008, at http://news.xinhuanet.com/mil/2008-04/26/content_8053374.htm. Also see "China Launches New Data Relay Satellite," Xinhua Net, July 12, 2011, at http://news.xinhuanet.com/english2010/sci/2011-07/12/c_13978690.htm.For an example of the data relay satellite being used for missile guidance, see Chen Lihu, Wang Shilian, Zhang Eryang, "Modeling And Simulation Of Missile Satellite-Missile Link Channel In Flying-Control Data-Link" [基于卫星中继的导弹飞控数据链链路分析], Systems Engineering And Electronics, 29(6), 2007. The chief designer of the satellite was Ye Peijian [叶培建].

154 Wu Ting-yong, Wu Shi-qi, Ling Xiang, "A MEO Tracking and Data Relay Satellite System Constellation Scheme for China," Journal of Electronic Science and Technology of China, December 2005.

155 Key engineers included Liu Jiyu, a leading engineer from the Wuhuan University of Survey and Mapping Technology. See "Liu Jiyu" [刘基余], University Network, November 2009, at http://www.daxue1g.cn/fengyunrenwu/200911/4570.html.

156 Liu Peixiang (ed.), "Our University Participates in Formal Establishment of Shenzhen Aerospace Dongfanghong Development Ltd." [我校参与组建的深圳航天东方红海特卫星有限公司正式成立], Harbin Industrial University News, March, 4, 2009, at http://news.hit.edu.cn/articles/2009/03-04/03163743.htm.

157 The Survey and Mapping Bureau MUCD is the 61081 Unit. The Bureau manages the China Satellite Navigation Positioning Management System [中国卫星航定位应用管理中心].

158 For overview of CASC microsatellite development, see [集团公司组织召开微小卫星关键技术研讨会], at China Space Network, May 6, 2011, at http://www.space.cetin.net.cn/index.asp?modelname=new_space%2Fnews_nr&FractionNo=&titleno=XWEN0000&recno=75869.

159 The China Academy of Sciences opened a microsatellite lab [中国科学院微小卫星重点实验室] in 2011. "CAS Microsatellite Key Laboratory Holds Inaugural Session of Academic Council" [中国科学院微小卫星重点实验室举行揭牌仪式暨学术委员会第一届第一次会议], CAS website, December 23, 2010, at http://www.cas.cn/hy/xshd/201012/t20101231_3052884.shtml. The NUAA project is the Tianxun-1 [天巡一号] intelligent network microsatellite system. See http://www.nuaa.edu.cn/nhb/997/b1.htm.

160 See "Aerospace Tsinghua 1 Satellite", ["航天清华" 一号卫星] under "CASIC Satellite Technology Ltd." official web site [航天科工卫星技术有限公司], at http://www.casic-sat.com.cn/operation4.asp.

161 For background on the CASIC role, see "CASIC Satellite Technology Ltd." official web site [航天科工卫星技术有限公司], at http://www.casic-sat.com.cn/abouts.asp, accessed on June 21, 2011.

162 See "Small Satellite R&D receives Breakthrough: China Successfully Launched "One Rocket, Two Stars", [中国成功发射"一箭双星"小卫星研制取得突破], *China News* [中新网], April 9, 2004, at http://news.tsinghua.edu.cn/publish/news/6661/2011/20110225231431312562162/20110225231431312562162_.html. See "The First Indigenously Made Nano-1 Satellite Has Been Launched Successfully", [第一颗自主研制的纳星一号发射成功], S&T Daily,, April 18, 2004, at http://www.stdaily.com/oldweb/gb/kjzg/2004-09/28/content_305818.htm.Also see http://www.smallsat.org/proceedings/13/tech-ix/ts-ix-3.pdf.

163 [我国首颗高校自主研制的微小卫星"试验卫星一号"发射成功], HIT website, July 7, 2008, at http://news.hit.edu.cn/articles/2008/07-07/07140722.htm. For background on the Shiyan-3, see [揭秘哈工大"试验卫星三号"], HIT website, November 11, 2008 at http://news.hit.edu.cn/articles/2008/11-11/11101604.htm.

164 Zhejiang University has been actively involved in research associated with strike technology, including the 863-801 and 863-805 programs.

165 See "Zhejiang University's Successful Launch of "Pixing-1A Satellite, Challenging Microsatellites" [浙江大学成功发射"皮星一号A"卫星 挑战微型小卫星], Zhejiang University, October 7, 2010, at http://memememama.cn/2010/1007/1334.html. Also see "Nation's First Kilogram-Level Micro-Satellite Operating Smoothly for Eight Days and Nights", [我国首颗公斤级微小卫星平稳运行八天八夜], Xinhua Network, September 30, 2010, at http://news.sina.com.cn/c/2010-09-30/222621204836.shtml. Also see http://www.most.gov.cn/eng/newsletters/2010/201010/t20101011_82540.htm.

166 For overview of the BX-1, see David Wright and Gregory Kulacki, "Chinese Shenzhou 7 'Companion Satellite' (BX-1), Union of Concerned Scientists, October 21, 2008, at http://www.ucsusa.org/assets/documents/nwgs/UCS-Shenzhou7-CompanionSat-10-21-08.pdf; and Brian Weeden, "China's BX-1 Microsatellite: a Litmus Test for Space Weaponization," *The Space Review*, October 20, 2008, at http://www.thespacereview.com/article/1235/1. The chief designer of the BX-1 was Zhu Zhencai.

167 Among various sources, see Peter B. de Selding, "Surrey To Build Three Optical Imaging Satellites for Chinese Firm," *Space News*, June 29, 2011, at http://www.spacenews.com/contracts/110629chinese-firm-orders-three-optical-imaging-satellites-from-surrey.html. The Chinese company is Twenty-First Century Aerospace Technology Co. Ltd. A ground station affiliated with the Beijing-1 satellite is collocated with a GSD Third Department Seventh Bureau facility in the northern Beijing suburb of Shangzhuang [上庄].

168 Greg Kulacki should be credited with highlighting the private nature of initial KT funding. Chinese references back up his assertions, and there appears to be a growing trend of initiatives being funded through venture capital.

169 Shi Fashu, "Kaituozhe-1 Solid Launch Vehicle Development Planning and Implementation," *China Aerospace* (*zhongguo hangtian*), August 2003, pp. 13-16.

170 Tian Zhiqiang , [小型固体运载火箭], *Space Exploration* [太空探索], October 2003. For background on the microsatellite payloads, see "KT-1PS/PS2/PS3载荷星", CASIC Satellite Technology Company website, undated, at http://www.casic-sat.com.cn/operation5.asp. The satellite passed its final factory certification on August 24, 2002, approximately five weeks before launch.

171 "China's First Four-Staged Solid Fuelled Launch Vehicle "KT-1" A Success" (*woguo diyixing siji quanguti yunzai huojian "kaituozhe yihao feixing shiyan rongde chenggong*), *China Space News*, September 19, 2003. The KT-1PS2 passed its factory certification on August 8, 2003, approximately five weeks before launch. The KT-1PS3 satellite passed factory certification on September 13, 2004.

[172] Gu Ti, "Kaituozhe: New Choice for Small Satellite Launches," *Aerospace China*, November 2002, p. 2. There are indications that the KT-2 has been re-designated as the KT-1B.

[173] For a general Chinese analysis, see Wang Shengkai, Quan Shouwen, Li Binhua, and Ma Qin, "Near Space and Near Space Flight Vehicles" (临近空间和临近空间飞行器),*CONMILIT*, (*Xiandai junshi*), 2007(7), pp. 36-39.

[174] Guo Weimin, Si Wanbing, Gui Qishan, and He Jiafan, "Coordination and Applicability of Near Space Flight Vehicles in Missile Warfare" [导弹作战中临近空间飞行器与航天器的协同应用], *Winged Missiles* [飞航导弹], May 2008.

[175] For a representative Second Artillery overview, see Li Chao, Luo Chuanyong and Wang Hongli, "Research into Near Space Flight Vehicle Applications for the Second Artillery" [近空间飞行器在第二炮兵部队的应用研究]; *Journal of Projectiles and Guidance*, January 2009; Tang Jiapeng, Guan Shixi, Ling Guilong, and Duan Na, "Study on Propulsion System of Near Space Vehicles," *Journal of Projectiles, Rockets, Missiles, and Guidance*, June 2009, pp. 145-148. Also see Li Zhen, Li Haiyang, and Yong En'mi, "Analysis of Trajectory Characteristics of Near Space Kinetic Weapons," *Journal of Projectiles, Rockets, Missiles, and Guidance*, June 2009, pp. 183-185.

[176] Wang Wenqin, Cai Jingye Cai, and Peng Qicong, "Conceptual Design Of Near-Space Synthetic Aperture Radar For High-Resolution And Wide-Swath Imaging," *Aerospace Science and Technology* (2009), pp. 1-8. Wang is from the University of Electronic Science and Technology of China (UESTC) and claims to be a leading advocate within China for near space SAR remote sensing.

[177] See Duan Dongbei, "Airship's R&D and Application to Aeronautics and Astronautics in China," briefing, CASIC Hunan Astronautic Industry Corporation, April 2008, at http://www.veatal.com/iso_album/duandongbei.pdf. AVIC's 605 Research Institute also is involved in airship R&D.

[178] See China's Defense White Paper (*China's National Defense in 2008*), January 20, 2009, at http://news.xinhuanet.com/english/2009-01/20/content_10688124_1.htm, accessed on August 29, 2009.

[179] For a detailed assessment of U.S. programs, see Xie Wu, "Four Major Challenges Facing An Accelerated US 'Prompt Global Strike" Program'," [美 "快速全球打击" 难获快速发展 面临四大难题], *China Daily*, June 11, 2010, at http://www.chinadaily.com.cn/hqjs/jsyw/2010-06-11/content_446614_2.html.

[180] "Establishing a National Aerospace Security System" [建立我国的空天安全体系], *Science News* [科学时报], February 24, 2002, at http://www.cas.cn/xw/zjsd/200202/t20020224_1683499.shtml

[181] For an excellent overview of the General Staff Department, see David Finklestein, "The General Staff Department of the Chinese People's Liberation Army: Organization, Roles, & Missions," in James C. Mulvenon and Andrew N.D. Yang, eds. *The People's Liberation Army as Organization: Reference Volume v1.0*, Santa Monica, CA: RAND, CF-182-NSRD, 2002, pp. 122-224.

[182] The command responsible for the Beidou ground segment is the 61081 Unit headquartered in Beijing.

[183] Yousaf Butt, "Effects of Chinese Laser Ranging on Imaging Satellites," Science and Global Security (17), pp. 20–35, 2009, at http://www.princeton.edu/sgs/publications/sgs/archive/17-1-Butt-Effects-of-Chinese.pdf. Reference to GSD laser ranging: http://info.edu.hc360.com/2009/03/11084170180.shtml.

[184] VLBI sites track space objects simultaneously via telescopes that are combined, emulating a telescope with a size equal to the maximum separation between the telescopes. Using ELINT methodology, VLBI measures the time difference of arrival (TDOA) of radio waves at separate antennas. Therefore, the GSD First Department Surveying Bureau likely has a close relationship with the GSD Fourth Department. VLBI sites, presumably subordinate to the brigade or regimental-level 61540 Unit, are in Shanghai Sheshan, Kunming, Guizhou

Qiaodongnan [黔东南] Huangping County, Wulumuqi Nanshan, and Beijing Miyun. See "PLA 61540 Unit Successfully Joins Moon Satellite Tracking and Control" [解放军61540部队成功参与探月卫星测控], China Surveying and Mapping Yearbook [中国测绘年鉴编], July 29, 2008, at http://zgchnj.sbsm.gov.cn/article//ljnjll/lbnj/tz/zdsj/200807/20080700039517.shtml. Other key GSD Surveying Bureau ground stations are located in Hainan.

[185] See GSD Weather and Oceanographic Space Weather Command Supports Shenzhou-8 Launch" [总参某气象水文空间天气总站保障 "神八" 发射], *Renminwang*, November 1, 2011, at http://military.people.com.cn/GB/172467/16087308.html. The space weather outfit may be the 61741 Unit. Space weather refers to adverse conditions on the sun, in solar wind, and in the Earth's magnetosphere, ionosphere, and thermosphere. These conditions can influence the performance and reliability of space-borne and ground-based systems and can endanger human life or health. These conditions can cause disruptions of satellite operations, communications, radar, navigation, high-altitude manned flight, and electrical power distribution grids.

[186] The military unit cover designator may be 61646. The institute [总参航天侦察局] manages a R&D center, which is directed by Zhou Zhixin [周志鑫]. For reference to Zhou, see [杜善义院士、曲久辉、栾恩杰和周志鑫校友获2009年度何梁何利奖], *Harbin Institute of Technology Today*, at http://today.hit.edu.cn/articles/2009/11-11/1115372591.htm. For reference to Zhou with the Second Department's Space Remote Sensing, see http://www.ciomp.cas.cn/jgsz/kyxt/klomt/sysgk_klomt/xswyh_klomt/. For reference to Zhou as 61646 Unit Deputy Bureau Director, see [胡锦涛签署通令给军队1个单位22名个人记功], at http://www.wpeu.net/html/china/2010/1225/18703.html.   Also see "Earthquake Prediction Institute Summary of Research on Emergency Respond to Yushu, Qinghai 7.1 Earthquake" [地震预测研究所应对青海玉树7.1级地震应急研究工作综述], China Earthquake Administration, May 11, 2010, at http://www.cea.gov.cn/manage/html/8a8587881632fa5c0116674a018300cf/_content/10_05/11/1273544138348.html. For reference to the 61646 Unit ground station (presumably an imagery downlink site), see [2007年度首都文明单位候选名单(1908个)], at http://jbhg.bjwmb.gov.cn/public/info_selinfo.asp?Info_ID=27680&Bar_ID=123.

[187] The 12th Bureau carries an cover designator of the 61486 Unit. For linkage of the 12th Bureau with the MUCD, see http://www.kshr.cn/ksasp/unit/SHOWEMPL.ASP?employee_id=660550. Third Department 12th Bureau Headquarters appears to be located on 46 Yuexiu Road in Shanghai's Zhabei District [闸北区粤秀路46号]. See http://www.isee.zju.edu.cn/attachments/2011-04/01-1302228510-41734.xls. The Jiangnan Institute of Remote Sensing Applications [江南遥感应用研究所] shares the same address. The 12th Bureau's former designation was the 57394 Unit.

[188] The 61486 Unit Commander, Senior Colonel Ju Qiansheng [巨乾生], has been affiliated with both the GSD Second Department Remote Sensing Institute and GSD Third Department's 12th Bureau. See "District Standing Committee, Deputy Mayor Yan Jianping Visits 61486 Unit for a Social Visit" [区委常委、副区长颜建平率队赴驻区61486部队开展军地互动联谊活动], February 8, 2010, at http://www.shmzj.gov.cn/gb/mzzbq/mzxw/zxxw/userobject1ai486.html.

[189] See Mark A. Stokes, Jenny Lin, and L.C. Russell Hsiao, *The Chinese People's Liberation Army Signals Intelligence and Cyber Reconnaissance Infrastructure* (Wash DC: Project 2049 Institute), November 11, 2011, p. 11, at http://project2049.net/documents/pla_third_department_sigint_cyber_stokes_lin_hsiao.pdf.

[190] "Ceremony Held for Establishment of the PLA Strategic Planning Department, Chairman Guo Boxiong Speaks" [解放军战略规划部成立大会举行 郭伯雄出席并讲话], *Xinhua*, November 22, 2011, at http://news.xinhuanet.com/mil/2011-11/22/c_111187194.htm.

[191] The first is a brigade-level organization based in Langfang with subordinate elements in Anhui, Jiangxi, and Shandong. The other, located on Hainan Island, appears to have either operational or experimental satellite jamming responsibilities. Director of the Hainan GSD 4th Department Regiment [61764 Unit] is Jin Guodong [靳国栋], as of 2009. One indication of the unit having satellite jamming responsibilities is the number of articles published by its members. See, for example, Li Bin and Jin Guodong, "Analysis on GPS Jamming" [浅析GPS干扰技术], *Electronic Countermeasures*, January 2009, pp. 39-42; Jin Guodong and Li Suoku, "On Broadband Communications Satellites [宽带卫星通信探析], *Electro-Optical Systems*, April 2008, pp. 16-31; and Zhang Ming and Li Suoku, "Space Information Warfare and International Space Law [空间信息作战与国际空间法], *Armament Command and Technology Academy Journal*, February 2003; and Xiang Hanfei, Li Suoku, and Han Honglin, "Analysis of GPS System Countermeasures," [GPS系统对抗若干分析], *Tracking and Communications*, October 2008.

[192] For an example of research supporting the Fourth Department ELINT mission, see Wu Shilong, Luo Jingqing, and Liu Youjun "Passive Location by Single Reconnaissance Satellite Based on Spatial Spectrum Estimation" [基于空间谱估计的单星侦察无源定位], *Shanghai Aerospace*, June 2005, at http://www.lw23.com/pdf_9588991b-8dd2-441a-baeb-3e576ca77a2f/lunwen.pdf. Gong Liangliang, Wang Yunliang, and Luo Jingqing, "Radar Electromagnetic Environment Simulation in Satellite Reconnaissance" [基于卫星侦察的雷达电磁环境仿真], *Modern Defense Technology* [现代防御技术], 2008 36(3), at http://d.wanfangdata.com.cn/periodical_xdfyjs200803031.aspx. The authors are from the GSD Fourth Department's Electronic Engineering Academy in Hefei. The Fourth Department oversees the GSD 54th Research Institute, which most likely provides engineering support, and also maintains close links with a number of China Electronic Technology Corporation (CETC) entities, including the 29th Research Institute in Chengdu, the 36th Research Institute in Jiaxing, and the 38th Research Institute in Hefei.

[193] For examples of U.S. overviews of China's space modernization, see Dean Cheng, "Prospects for China's Military Space Efforts," in Roy Kamphausen, David Lai, and Andrew Scobell (eds), *Beyond The Strait: PLA Missions Other Than Taiwan* (Carlisle PA: 2009), pp. 211-252, at http://www.strategicstudiesinstitute.army.mil/pdffiles/pub910.pdf; Eric Hagt and Matthew Durnin, "China's Antiship Ballistic Missile: Developments and Missing Links," *Naval War College Review* 62, no. 4 (Autumn 2009), pp. 87–115; Andrew S. Erickson, "Eyes in the Sky," *U.S. Naval Institute Proceedings*, Vol. 136, No. 4 (April 2010), pp. 36-41; Gregory Kulacki and Jeffrey G. Lewis, *A Place for One's Mat: China's Space Program, 1956–2003* (Cambridge, MA: American Academy of Arts and Sciences, 2009), at http://www.amacad.org/publications/spaceChina.pdf; Kevin Pollpeter, "The Chinese Vision of Space Military Operations," pp, 329-369, in *China's Revolution in Doctrinal Affairs: Emerging Trends in the Operational Art of the Chinese People's Liberation Army*, edited by James Mulvenon and David Finklestein, CNA Corporation, Virginia. December 2005, at http://www.defensegroupinc.com/cira/pdf/doctrinebook_ch9.pdf; Larry M. Wortzel, *The Chinese People's Liberation Army and Space Warfare: Emerging United States-China Military Competition* (Wash DC: American Enterprise Institute, 2007), at http://www.aei.org/paper/26977; Michael P. Pillsbury, "An Assessment of China's Anti-Satellite and Space Warfare Programs, Policies, and Doctrines," Report for the U.S.-China Economic and Security Review Commission, January 19, 2007, at http://www.uscc.gov/researchpapers/2007/FINAL_REPORT_1-19-2007_REVISED_BY_MPP.pdf; Alanna Krolikowski, "China's Civil and Commercial Space Activities and their Implications," Testimony before the U.S.-China Economic and Security Review Commission Hearing on the "Implications of China's Military and Civil Space Programs, May 11, 2011, at http://www.gwu.edu/~spi/assets/docs/11_05_11_krolikowski_testimony.pdf; Dean Cheng "China's Space Program: Civilian, Commercial, and Military Aspects," CNA Corporation Conference Report, May 2006; Phillip C. Saunders, "China's Future in Space: Implications for U.S. Security," *AdAstra*, Spring

2005, pp. 21-23, at http://www.space.com/adastra/china_implications_0505.html; and Joan Johnson-Freese, China's Space Ambitions, *IFRI Proliferation Paper*, Summer 2007, at www.ifri.org/downloads/China_Space_Johnson_Freese.pdf.

194 For a primer, see *Counterspace Operations*, Air Force Doctrine Document 2-2.1, August 2, 2004, at http://www.dtic.mil/doctrine/jel/service_pubs/afdd2_2_1.pdf.

195 For an excellent overview of the challenges in leveraging Chinese language materials and an historical account of public references to China's ASAT program, see Gregory Kulacki, "Anti-Satellite (ASAT) Technology in Chinese Open-Source Publications," Global Security Program, Union of Concerned Scientists, July 1, 2009, at http://www.ucsusa.org/assets/documents/nwgs/Kulacki-Chinese-ASAT-Literature-6-10-09.pdf.

196 "Annual Threat Assessment of the Intelligence Community for the Senate Select Committee on Intelligence," 12 February 2009, p. 23.

197 For an early assessment of overall requirements of air and space defense, see Yin Xingliang, Future Air and Space Defense Missile System Architecture and Technology" [未来防空防天导弹体系结构与技术], *China Aerospace*, January 2001, at http://www.space.cetin.net.cn/docs/ht0101/ht010114.htm. Born in 1953, Yin Xingliang passed away in December 2010.

198 For reference to the action plan and space-based surveillance system, see "China Decides upon Three Major Engineering Programs for 2006-2020 Space Debris Action Plan" [中国确定2006至2020年空间碎片行动计划三大工程], December 25, 2003, at http://www.cnsa.gov.cn/n615708/n676979/n676983/n886611/66292.html.

199 Chen Weixia, "Our Nation's First Successful Satellite Avoidance of Space Debris," *China Aerospace Paper* (October 30, 2009) http://www.9ifly.cn/sub/viewthread.php?tid=2090.

200 See, for example, [新华日报：紫金山天文台监测空间碎片，为神七护驾], CAS website, September 2008, at http://www.cas.cn/jzd/jtjzt/jsqzt/200809/t20080926_1728217.shtml. For reference to the action plan and space-based surveillance system, see "China Decides upon Three Major Engineering Programs for 2006-2020 Space Debris Action Plan" [中国确定2006至2020年空间碎片行动计划三大工程], December 25, 2003, at http://www.cnsa.gov.cn/n615708/n676979/n676983/n886611/66292.html. Also see http://www.pmo.ac.cn/jgsz/gctz/yagcz/.

201 See Zhang Guangyi et. al., *Space Surveillance Phased Array Radar* [空间探测相控阵雷达], (Beijing: Science Press, 2001), pp. 1-14 For reference to GSD laser ranging, see "China's First Successful Laser Ranging Telescope Installed" [我国首台激光测距天文望远镜安装成功], China Instrument Association website, March 11, 2009, at http://info.edu.hc360.com/2009/03/110841170180.shtml. For an overview of satellite range finding, see Yousaf Butt, "Effects of Chinese Laser Ranging on Imaging Satellites," Science and Global Security (17), pp. 20–35, 2009, at http://www.princeton.edu/sgs/publications/sgs/archive/17-1-Butt-Effects-of-Chinese.pdf.

202 "Establishing a National Aerospace Security System" [建立我国的空天安全体系], *Science News* [科学时报], February 24, 2002, at http://www.cas.cn/xw/zjsd/200202/t20020224_1683499.shtml

203 See, for example, "Present and Future of Foreign Air and Space Defense Equipment", [國外防空防天裝備發展現狀與趨勢], *Aerospace Electronic Warfare*, at http://d.wanfangdata.com.cn/periodical_htdzdk201003002.aspx. Also see "PLA Air Defense Unit Has Anti-Missile Capabilities, Changing Air Defense" [解放军防空部队具备反导能力, 将向防天转变], 猎讯军情网, June 8, 2011, at http://www.1n0.net/Article/zhjs/114708.html.

204 For a detailed assessment of U.S. programs, see Xie Wu, "Four Major Challenges Facing An Accelerated US 'Prompt Global Strike" Program'," [美"快速全球打击"难获快速发展 面临四大难题], *China Daily*, June 11, 2010, at http://www.chinadaily.com.cn/hqjs/jsyw/2010-06-11/content_446614_2.html.

205 The solid-fueled launch vehicle boosts an unmanned, maneuverable, hypersonic flight vehicle into near space, which glides back through the atmosphere at speeds exceeding Mach 20. The launch vehicle also could be capable of launching microsatellites into space on short notice. See Xin Dingding, "US Spacecraft Sparks Arms Race Concerns," *China Daily*, April 24, 2010, at http://www2.chinadaily.com.cn/world/2010-04/24/content_9770149.htm.

206 Taiwan's first generation remote sensing satellite, the Formosat-2, was launched from Vandenberg AFB in 2004 and was to complete its intended service life in 2009. Proposed programs under debate within the Legislative Yuan included a Formosat-2 follow-on and a broadband communications satellite. Regardless of PLA intent, the ASAT test appeared to be one factor in a legislative freeze on Taiwan satellite programs. Indications exist that Taiwan's remote sensing satellite acquisition may be proceeding after an extended delay. For an overviews of China's ASAT program and test, see Ian Easton, "The Great Game in Space: China's Evolving ASAT Weapons Programs and Their Implications for Future U.S. Strategy," Project 2049 *Occasional Paper*, June 24, 2009; Kevin Pollpeter, Motives and Implications Behind China's ASAT Test, Jamestown China Brief, Volume: 7 Issue: 2, May 9, 2007, at http://www.jamestown.org/single/?no_cache=1&tx_ttnews%5Btt_news%5D=4022; Richard Fisher, Jr, "China's Direct Ascent ASAT," International Assessment and Strategy Center, January 20, 2007, at http://www.strategycenter.net/research/pubID.142/pub_detail.asp; Jeffrey Lewis, Gregory Kulacki, and Theresa Hitchens, "A Different View of China's ASAT Test," Carnegie Endowment for International Peace, November 13, 2007, at http://www.carnegieendowment.org/2007/11/13/different-view-of-china-s-asat-test/l9n; and Eric Hagt, "China's ASAT Test: Strategic Response," *China Security*, Winter 2007, pp. 31- 51, at http://www.wsichina.org/cs5_3.pdf.

207 For an excellent and reasonable analysis of the January 2010 missile defense interceptor test by a well regarded independent Chinese military-technical analyst, see KKTT, "A Preliminary Analysis of China's Ground-Based Mid-Course Missile Defense Interceptor Technology Test" [我国"陆基中段反导拦截技术试验"初步分析], KKTT blog, January 12, 2010, at http://liuqiankktt.blog.163.com/blog/static/12126421120100129195498/. Also see Mark A. Stokes, *China's Strategic Modernization: Implications for U.S. National Security* (Carlisle, PA: Army War College, 1999), p. 115; and Ian Easton, The Great Game in Space: China's Evolving ASAT Weapons Programs and Their Implications for Future U.S. Strategy, The Project 2049 Institute Occasional Paper, June 24, 2009.

208 Chinese engineers familiar with the space program speculated on a technical bulletin board site that the KKV "space interceptor" may have been a 25-35 kg microsatellite equipped with experimental imaging infrared and millimeter wave terminal homing package. Key 863-409 group members include Chen Dingchang (陈定昌), Huang Chunping (黄春平) from Harbin Institute of Technology, Yang Guoguang (杨国光) from Zhejiang University, and Xiao Wen (肖文) from the CASC First Academy, who served as deputy designer of the 409 KKV. Xiao Wen specializes in fiber optic gyroscope and other optoelectronic technologies. Chen Dingchang is said to have served as the chief designer of the ASAT/missile defense interceptor KKV, with Zhang Yiqun [张奕群] as the deputy chief designer for the KKV sub-system. Zhang is from the Second Academy's Second Design Department. A senior designer from the CASIC Fourth Academy's Fourth Design Department, Zheng Chenghuo [郑盛火], is said to be leading the development of the solid launch vehicle sub-system. CASC's Huang Chunping [黄春平] played a role in the early phases of the program, and became involved in the manned space program. Shi Xiaoping (史小平) from Harbin Institute of Technology conducted a series of modeling studies. More players included Lin Xiangdi (林祥棣) from the Southwest University of Science and Technology, Wan Ziming (万自明) from the Second Academy Second Design Department, and Zhou Jun (周军) from Northwest Polytechnical University, who played a leading role in establishing his university's Opto-Electronic and Imaging Precision Guidance Lab [光电和图像精确制导实验室]. See

"Report on Recent Research Advances in Micro-Optics" ['微光学的应用及其最新研究进展' 学术报告], Announcement, China Jiliang University, College of Information Engineering, September 11, 2006, at http://xxgcxy.cjlu.edu.cn/ReadNews.asp?NewsID=609.

209 For a comprehensive discussion of PLA operational space theory, see Larry Wortzel, "The Chinese People's Liberation Army and Space Warfare: Emerging United States-China Military Competition," *AEI Online*, October 17, 2007, at http://www.aei.org/papers/foreign-and-defense-policy/regional/asia/the-chinese-peoples-liberation-army-and-space-warfare/.

210 "Establishing a New Concept for Air Defense Operations Under Informationization Conditions" [确立信息化条件下防空作战新观念], *PLA Daily*, June 21, 2005, at http://www.china.com.cn/military/txt/2005-06/21/content_5894857.htm.

211 "Establishing a National Aerospace Security System" [建立我国的空天安全体系], *Science News* [科学时报], February 24, 2002, at http://www.cas.cn/xw/zjsd/200202/t20020224_1683499.shtml; "Xu Qiliang: The Chinese Air Force Must Have an Aerospace Security Perspective" [许其亮：中国空军必须树立空天安全观], Xinhua, November 1, 2009, at http://mil.news.sina.com.cn/2009-11-01/1424572155.html; Zhu Hui [朱晖], "China's Aerospace Security Facing Threat of Full Range of Stealthy Unmanned Vehicles and Other Weapon Systems" [我国空天安全面临隐形战机无人机等武器威胁], *PLA Daily*, December 3, 2009, at http://mil.eastday.com/m/20091203/u1a4853820.html; and "PLAAF Deputy Commander Chen Xiaogong Calls for Attention to Aerospace Security" [解放军空军副司令员陈小工呼吁关注空天安全], *China News Service*, March 9, 2010, at http://military.people.com.cn/GB/1076/52984/11107476.html; and Zhong Shan, "Discussion of Information Age of the Aerospace Century" [论信息时代的空天世纪], *China Space News*, February 4, 2010, at http://www.china-spacenews.com/n435777/n435778/n674308/65983.html.

212 "General Xu Qiliang: The PLA Air Force Will Develop an Integrated Air and Space Operational Capability" [许其亮上将：中国空军将发展空天一体作战能力], *Xinhua*, November 11, 2009, at http://mil.news.sina.com.cn/2009-11-05/1743572706.html.

213 See Shan Xu, "The Chinese Air Force's "Path of Leapfrogging" [中国空军的"跨越之路"], Oriental Outlook [瞭望东方周刊], August 5, 2010, at http://www.lwdf.cn/oriental/cover_story/20100805141022999.htm.

214 http://news.ifeng.com/mainland/detail_2010_09/14/2512164_0.shtml.

215 See Liu Yazhou Wenzhai at http://wenku.baidu.com/view/ce7fa62458fb770bf78a5534.html, p. 8.

216 Yu Jixun (ed.), *Second Artillery Campaign Science* [dierpaobing zhanyixue] (Beijing: National Defense University Press, 2004), pp. 70, 75, and 142.

217 For one discussion of use of ballistic missiles, see Paul B. Stares, Space and national security (Wash DC: Brookings Institution, 1987), pp. 97-99.

218 Li Guoqiang [李國強], "New Strategy of the PLA Air Force" [中国空军新战略], *Wenhuipo*, (Hong Kong), November 26, 2009, at http://paper.wenweipo.com/2009/11/26/PL0911260003.htm, accessed on May 3, 2010.

219 Zhang Wei, "Discussion of Accelerating Air and Space Integration Equipment Development" [试论加快空天一体战装备发展], *Ground Based Air Defense Weapon Systems* [地面防空武器], January 2003, pp. 2-6. Zhang Wei [张伟] served as Director, PLAAF Equipment Department R&D Department. The Academy's Director is Lu Gang [吕刚]; its Senior Engineer is Gan Xiaohua [甘晓华], an engine R&D specialist. Zhang Wei now serves as Deputy Director, PLAAF Equipment Department.

220 Among U.S. sources, see Roger Cliff, "The Development of China's Air Force Capabilities," Testimony presented before the U.S.-China Economic and Security Review, Commission, May 20, 2010; and Wayne A. Ulman, "China's Emergent Military Aerospace and Commercial Aviation Capabilities," Testimony before the U.S. – China Economic and Security Review Commission, 20 May 2010, http://www.uscc.gov/hearings/2010hearings/written_testimonies/10_05_20_wrt/10_05_20_ulman_statement.php.

221 Chen Hongbo and Yang Di, "Reentry Maneuver Control Strategy Study of Common Aero Vehicle," Systems and Control in Aerospace and Astronautics, (Shenzhen ISSCAA 2006), 19-21 Jan. 2006, page(s): 638-642. The authors are from the Harbin Institute of Technology. Also see Zhai Hua and Zhou Bozhao, "Adjustable Range Trajectory Design with Multiple Constraints for Precision Guided Vehicles," Systems and Control in Aerospace and Astronautics, (ISSCAA 2006), 19-21 Jan. 2006, page(s): 1-4. The authors are from the National University of Defense Technology; and Zhou Wenya, Chen Hongbo, and Yang Di, "Entry Guidance for Common Aero Vehicle," Systems and Control in Aerospace and Astronautics, 2nd International Symposium on Systems and Control in Aerospace and Astronautics (ISSCAA), Shenzhen, China, 19-21 Jan. 2006, page(s): 4-6. Chen Hongbo is from CASC First Academy. Others are from the Harbin Institute of Technology. Another is Wang Yunliang, Tang Wei, Zhang Yong, and Li Weiji, "Aerodynamic Configuration Optimization of a Common Aero Vehicle," Journal of Astronautics, July 2006, funded by a Chinese Natural Sciences grant. Also see Zhao Ruian, "Concept of Orbital Ballistic Missiles," Aerospace China, Issue 1, 2004.

222 "Background Information on Qirun Dong, Zhu Xuejun, Fan Shiwei" [齐润东、祝学军、樊士伟基本情况及简要事迹],China Society of Astronautics, September 16, 2010 at http://www.csaspace.org.cn/CMS/xhdt/ArticleShow.asp?ArticleID=877. Born in Shenyang in December 1962, Zhu Xuejun graduated from NUDT's Automated Control Department in 1984 [防科技大学自动控制系]. In 1997, she led a conceptual [论证] design study on a system. From the First Academy's design department, Zhu was assigned as the chief designer of a missile system in 1999, most likely the DF-15A.

223 For further background, see Mark Stokes, China's Evolving Conventional Strategic Strike Capability: The Anti-Ship Ballistic Missile Challenge to U.S. Maritime Operations in the Western Pacific and Beyond, Project 2049 Institute Occasional Paper, September 2009.

224 For general discussions on terminal guidance systems, see Zhang Yiguang and Zhou Chengping, "Technological Trends Associated with Surface-to-Surface Ballistic Missile Precision Guidance" (didi dandao daodan sixian yuancheng qingque daji de jishu qujing), Tactical Missile Control Technology (Zhanshu daodan kongzhi jishu), 2004(4), pp. 58-60. The authors are from from the 066 Base's design department and Huazhong University.

225 This observation is credited to Richard P. Hallion, "The X-Vehicles: Advancing the Limits of Technology," presentation to the Joint NASA-USAF-AIAA X-Vehicle Symposium, 21 May 2002, at http://www.aiaa.org/documents/conferences/Presentations/Hallion.pdf. For a discussion on possible designs, see Richard Fisher, Jr, "China's Space Plane Program," International Assessment and Strategy Center, July 27, 2011, at http://www.strategycenter.net/research/pubID.253/pub_detail.asp.

226 226 For a good overview of the Prompt Global Strike program and more specifically the deployment of conventional ballistic missiles, see Bruce M. Sugden. "Speed Kills: Analyzing the Deployment of Conventional Ballistic Missiles," International Security Volume 34, Issue 1 (2009), pp. 113-146.

227 Key players involved in technology policy oversight include Cui Erjie [崔尔杰] from the 701st Research Institute, Zhang Litong [张立同], a senior composite materials expert with NUAA, Wu Hongxin [吴宏鑫] from the CASC Fifth Academy's 502nd Research Institute, Nie Haitao [聂海涛] from AVIC's 611 Research Institute, re-entry vehicle specialist An Fuxing [安复兴] from the CASC First Academy's 14th Research Institute, scramjet engine specialist

Wang Zhenguo [王振国] from the PLA National University of Defense Technology, and senior force development planner Zhu Rongchang [朱荣昌] associated with the PLAAF Headquarters Department Military Theory Department [空军司令部军事理论研究部]. See "Conference Opens on Near Space Flight Vehicle Development Trends and Issues in Major Basic Technology Program" [临近空间飞行器的发展趋势和重大基础科学问题研讨会在京召开], National Natural Science Foundation, May 12, 2006, at http://www.nsfc.gov.cn/Portal0/InfoModule_375/1111.htm.

228 U.S. media reported the ASBM as having characteristics of a cruise missile. See Christopher P. Cavas, "Missile Threat Helped Drive DDG Cut," *Defense News*, August 4, 2008. For references to the Qian Xuesen trajectory, see Gu Wenjin, Yu Jinyong, and Zhao Hongchao, "New Concept of M-Type Missile Trajectory," *Journal of Naval Aviation Academy*, 2004, Vol. 19, No. 2. Also see Hu Zhengdong et.al, "Trajectory Performance Analysis and Optimization Design for Hypersonic Skip Vehicle," *Journal of Astronautics*, 2008 (1), pp. 66-71. Also see Xu Wei, Shen Pizhong, and Xia Zhixun, "Integrated Design and Optimization for Boost-Glide Missiles," *Journal of Solid Rocket Technology*, Vol. 31 No. 4, pp. 317-320; Yang En'mi, Tang Guojin, and Chen Lei, "Schematic Study for Mid-Course Trajectories for Boost-Glide Missiles," *Journal of National University of Defense Technology*, Vol 28, Issue 6, 2006; and Li Yu, Cui Naigang, Guo Jifeng, "Development and Key Technology Analysis of Boost-Glide Missile," *Tactical Missile Technology*, 2008 (5); and Guo Xingling and Zhang Heng, "An Analysis of the Maximum Time Rates of Heat of Long-Range Boost Glide Flight," *Journal of Astronautics*, 2008,29(3), pp. 783-788. Also see Li Yu, Yang Zhihong, and Cui Naigang, "Study on Optimal Trajectory for Boost-Glide Ballistic Missiles," *Journal of Astronautics*, January 2008, Vol 29, No.1, pp. 66-71. Li Yu, Cui Naigang, and Guo Jifeng, "Development and Key Technology Analysis of Boost-Glide Missile," *Tactical Missile Technology*, May 2008.

229 The boost-glide concept was first developed by Eugene Sanger and other German aerospace engineers in the 1930s and refined by Dr. Qian Xuesen, the father of China's space and missile program, while at the U.S. Jet Propulsion Laboratory (JPL) in 1951. In Sanger's concept, a launch vehicle would propel itself to the upper atmosphere then glide with no power until it hit denser air. It then would use kinetic energy to skip off the atmosphere back up to higher altitudes, similar to a stone skipping along water. Each skip reduces the available energy until it glides toward its target. Sanger calculated that a missile launched from Nazi Germany would require three skips to strike a target in the eastern United States. The Russians reportedly flight tested a similar boost-glide vehicle in 2005. The "skipping" also could involve energy management or "phugoid" porpoise-like measures in which the missile pitches up and climbs then pitches down and descends.

230 Guan Shiyi, "Regarding Qian Xuesen's New Concept for Ballistic Trajectory," *Winged Missiles Journal (feihang daodan)*, 2003, Issue 1, pp. 1-4. For an alternative concept, see Gu Liangxian, Gong Chunlin, and Wu Wuhua, "Design and Optimization of Wavy Trajectory for Ballistic Missiles," *Acta Armamentarii*, Vol. 26, No. 3. May 2005, pp. 353-355.

231 Zhan Hao, Sun Dechuan, and Xia Lu, "Preliminary Design for Soaring Hypersonic Cruise Vehicle," *Journal of Solid Rocket Technology*, Vol. 30, No. 1, 2007. The authors are also from the Northwest Polytechnical University's College of Astronautics.

232 Xu Wei, Sun Pizhong, and Xia Zhixun, "Integration Design and Optimization for Boost Glide Missile" (助推-滑翔导弹总体一体化优化设计), *Journal of Solid Rocket Technology*, Vol 31, No. 4, 2008, p. 319.

233 For one of the best overviews, see Gao Feng, "The Application of Radar Homing Technology in Long-range Precision Guided Missiles" (雷达寻的技术在远程精确制导导弹中的应用) *Aerospace Shanghai (Shanghai hangtian)*, 2004 (5), pp. 25-29. Gao is from the Shanghai Academy of Space Technology (CASC Eighth Academy) 802nd Research Institute. This organization specializes in missile guidance systems. Among other various sources, see Zou Weibao, Ren Sicong, and Li Zhilin, "Application of SAR in Combined Navigation System for Vehicle," *Aerospace Control*, Issue 1, 2002; Jiang Jinlong, Mu Rongjun, Cui Naigang, "Application of SAR in Terminal Guidance of Ballistic Missile," *Journal of Ballistics*, Issue 2, 2008; and Zhang Junchang, Hou Yibin, Zou Weibao, and Gao

Shesheng, "Study of Tactical Ballistic Missile with Integrated Guidance System SINS/GNSS/SAR," *Journal of Projectiles, Rockets, Missiles and Guidance*, No. 4, 2000. For a design study associated with a DSP for SAR signal processing (TS203), see He Zhiming, Zhu Jiang, and Zhou Bo, "Research on Real Time Signal Processing of Missile-Borne SAR System," *Journal of Electronics and Information Technology*, April 2008, Vol. 30, Issue 4. The authors are from UESTC. CASIC's Third Academy 35th Research Institute also is said to be involved in missile-borne (弹载) SAR guidance R&D, as are engineers from the PLA Navy and PLA Air Force. For the aviation community, the Leihua Electronic Technology Research Institute in Wuxi appears to be doing work in use of SAR for air-to-air missiles.

234 For general overviews, see Wang Qiang, Huang Jianchong, and Jiang Qiuxi, "The Chief Development Trends of Synthetic Aperture Radar" (合成孔径雷达的主要发展方向),*Modern Defense Technology*, April 2007, pp. 81-88. The authors are from the PLA's Institute of Electronic Engineering in Hefei, Anhui province. Also see Qin Yuliang, Wang Jiantao, Wang Hongqiang, and Li Xiang, "Overview of Missile-Borne Synthetic Aperture Radar" (弹载合成孔径雷达技术研究综述), *Signal Processing (xinhao chuli)*, April 2009, pp. 630-635. The authors are from the National University of Defense Technology (NUDT), which hosts a National Laboratory for Precision Guidance and Automated Target Recognition (精确制导自动目标识别国家重点实验室).

235 See for example Chen Haidong and Yu Menglun, "Concept for Maneuvering Re-Entry Vehicle Integrated Guidance" (机动再入飞行器的复合制导方案研究), *Journal of Astronautics (Yuhang xuebao)*, Vol. 22, No. 5 (Sep 01), pp. 72.76.

236 Zhang Hongrong, Tang Yuesheng, Wu Guan, and Long Sun, "SAR Deceptive Jamming Signal Simulation," conference paper presented at the 1st Asian and Pacific Conference on Synthetic Aperture Radar, 2007. APSAR 2007. Volume , Issue , 5-9 Nov. 2007, pp. 61-64. The authors are from the East China Research Institute of Electronic Engineering in Hefei.

237 In one Chinese analysis, the ASBM radar is viewed as sophisticated and costly as the AN/APG-77 active electronically scanned array (AESA) radar. With the radar accounting for about half, the authors estimate that the unit cost of an ASBM including the launcher would U.S. $5-10.5 million. See Qiu and Long, "A Discussion of China's Development of an Anti-Ship Ballistic Missile," *Modern Ships (Xiandai jianchuan)*, 2006 Issue 12(B); and Qiu and Long, "930 Seconds – A Discussion on China's Development of an Anti-Ship Ballistic Missile (Operational Scenario)," *Modern Ships*, 2007 Issue 01(B).

238 While unclear at the present time, it appears that R&D on ground and air-launched variants of the DH-10 were conducted in parallel. Both variants appear to have been tested in Summer and Fall 2003. The CASIC Third Academy design team appears to have included Liu Yongcai [刘永才] as chief designer, Zheng Riheng [郑日恒] as engine sub-system designer; Feng Dawei [冯大伟] as control sub-system designer; and Zou Zhiqin [邹志勤] as INS sub-system designer.

239 "Yang Baokui: Leapfrogging of China's Precision Weapons R&D" [杨宝奎 ：中国精确制导武器研制实现技术跨越], China Academy of Sciences website, April 19, 2004, in http://www.cas.cn/xw/zjsd/200906/t20090608_644604.shtml.

240 Wayne A. Ulman, "China's Emergent Military Aerospace and Commercial Aviation Capabilities," Testimony before the U.S. – China Economic and Security Review Commission, 20 May 2010, http://www.uscc.gov/hearings/2010hearings/written_testimonies/10_05_20_wrt/10_05_20_ulman_statement.php.

241 Marcia S. Smith, "Space Launch Vehicles: Government Activities, Commercial Competition, and Satellite Exports," *Issue Brief for Congress*, 3 Feb 2003, 6 July 2011, <http://fpc.state.gov/documents/organization/17353.pdf>.

242 See "2006 China's Aerospace White Paper" [2006年中国的航天白皮书全文], China National Space Administration [国家航天局], October 12, 2006, at http://www.cnsa.gov.cn/n615708/n620168/n750545/79483.html.

243 See "S.S. Razov, Special Envoy from Russia to China, Speaks at a Meet-and-Greet with Students from International Economic and Trade [俄罗斯驻中国特命全权大使S.S.拉佐夫在与对外经济贸易大学同学的见面会上发言], The Embassy of the Russian Federation in the People's Republic of China, March 24, 2011, at http://www.russia.org.cn/chn/2735/31293295.print, accessed on June 26, 2011.

244 Antoly Zek, "Cooperation with China," 13 June 2011, 24 June 2011 <http://www.russianspaceweb.com/luna_glob.html>.

245 See "Ma Xing-rui Meets with Perminov, Chief of Russian Space Agency [马兴瑞会见俄罗斯航天局局长佩尔米诺夫], CASC official website, July 6, 2009, at http://www.spacechina.com/gjjlyhz_zyhd_Details.shtml?recno=60931.

246 See "China National Space Administration Delegation to Russian Space Agency" [中国国家航天局代表团访俄罗斯航天局], China Great Wall Industry Cooperation official website, December 3, 2010, at http://cn.cgwic.com/news/2010/1203_Delegation_China_National_Space_Administration_Visited_Russian_Federal_Space_Agency.html, accessed on June 26, 2011.

247 The specific entity is the 7801 Research Institute. See "China and Russia Sign Business Agreement for Technological Cooperation Program" [中俄技术合作项目在长沙签订商务合同], CASIC Website, January 5, 2011, at http://www.casic.com.cn/web82/subject/n1/n82/n107/n163/c238011/content.html.

248 See Vladimir Isachenkov, "Russian Space Exec Convicted for Aiding China," Associated Press, December 3, 2007, at http://www.msnbc.msn.com/id/22082431/ns/technology_and_science-space/t/russian-space-exec-convicted-aiding-china/.

249 See, for example, "Ukraine and China Sign Space Cooperation Program until 2015," Interfax Ukraine, September 3, 2010, at http://www.kyivpost.com/news/business/bus_general/detail/81018/.

250 See "China and Ukraine to Establish Strategic Partnership Relations" [中国乌克兰或建战略伙伴关系], Oriental Morning Post [东方早报], June 20, 2011, at http://epaper.dfdaily.com/dfzb/html/2011-06/20/content_495206.htm, accessed on June 27, 2011.

251 "Sino-Kazakh relations", [中哈双边关系], China Ministry of Foreign Affairs Website [外交部网站], February 28, 2008, at http://politics.people.com.cn/GB/8198/136846/136848/8218969.html.

252 See "Ma Xingrui Meets Chief of Kazakh Space Agency" [马兴瑞会见哈萨航天局局长], China Space News [中国航天报], May 6, 2011, at http://www.spacechina.com/gjjlyhz_zyhd_Details.shtml?recno=75667; and "Kazakh Guests Visit China Aerospace Science and Technology Corporation (CASC), [哈萨克斯坦客人来访航天科技集团], China Space News [中国航天报], March 19, 2010, article posted at http://www.spacechina.com/gjjlyhz_zyhd_Details.shtml?recno=66179.

253 Among various sources, see "China and France Discuss Space Cooperation" [中法航天洽谈合作], China Space News, April 8, 2011.

254 Liu Jiyuan, "Strengthening Space Cooperation, Looking Forward to the 21st Century," Zhongguo Hangtian, June 1996, at http://www.space.cetin.net.cn/docs/HTM-E/002.HTM; and "China Developing Space Solar Telescope" [中国正研制空间太阳望远镜], Nanjing Daily, March 11, 2009, at http://njrb.njnews.cn/html/2009-03/11/content_213032.htm.

255 See "Double Star Overview," European Space Agency website, April 13, 2007, at http://www.esa.int/esaSC/120381_index_0_m.html.

256 [玻利维亚通信卫星及地面应用系统项目正式签], *China Space News*, December 15, 2010; and See Evan Ellis, "Advances in China – Latin America Space Cooperation," Jamestown China Brief, Volume. 10, Issue. 14, July 9, 2010.

257 "China Successfully Launches NigComSat-1R for Nigeria," CGWIC news release, December 20, 2011, at http://www.cgwic.com/news/2011/1220_China_successfully_launches_NigComSat-1R_for_Nigeria.html.

258 See "Vice-Chairman Zhang Xiaodong Attends China-Indonesia Business Forum" [张晓东副总裁出席中国—印度尼西亚商务论坛], China Great Wall Industry Corporation, November 12, 2010, at http://cn.cgwic.com/news/2010/1112_Indonesia-China_Business_Forum.html.

259 "CGWIC Signs LaoSat-1 Communications Satellite Contract," CGWIC website, February 25, 2010, at http://www.cgwic.com/news/2010/0225_LaoSat-1.html.

260 See "Environmental Monitoring Satellite A Receiving Station for Thailand: A "Zero Breakthrough" for Export of Remote Sensing Ground Station System" [环境监测A星泰国接收站交付: 我国实现卫星遥感地面接收站整套系统出口"零的突破"], CASC website [中国航天科技集团公司], April 8, 2011, at http://www.spacechina.com/gjjlyhz_zyhd_Details.shtml?recno=74758.

261 Doug Messier, "Chinese Space Leader Calls for Cooperation as Congress Says No," *Parabolic Arc*, 15 April 2011, at http://www.parabolicarc.com/2011/04/15/chinese-space-leader-calls-cooperation-congress .

262 Jeffrey Logan, "China's Space Program: Options for U.S.-China Cooperation," CRS Report for Congress, 29 Sept 2009, 6 July 2011, <http://www.fas.org/sgp/crs/row/RS22777.pdf>.
263 "Administrator Griffin Visits China," Transcript of NASA Press Conference in Beijing, NASA Office of Public Affairs, September 25, 2006, at http://www.spaceref.com/news/viewsr.html?pid=22184.

264 Joan Johnson-Freese, ""US-China Space Cooperation: Congress' Pointless Lockdown," *China-US Focus*, 10 June 2011, at http://www.chinausfocus.com/peace-security/us-china-space-cooperation-congress%E2%80%99-pointless-lockdown.

265 For an overview of the costs and benefits of U.S.-China space cooperation, see Jeffrey Logan, "China's Space Program: Options for U.S.-China Cooperation," *CRS Report for Congress*, 29 Sept 2009, at http://www.fas.org/sgp/crs/row/RS22777.pdf. Also see Jeffrey Logan, "China's Space Program: Options for U.S.-China Cooperation," *CRS Report for Congress*, 29 Sept 2009, 6 July 2011, <http://www.fas.org/sgp/crs/row/RS22777.pdf>. Also see "The Future of U.S.-China Space Cooperation," *NASA*, 20 July 2006, at http://www.nasa.gov/offices/oce/appel/ask-academy/issues/ask-oce/AO_1-10_F_future.html.

www.ingramcontent.com/pod-product-compliance
Lightning Source LLC
Chambersburg PA
CBHW082145290526
45794CB00008B/3166